CALSO COOKS
REAL FOOD MADE EASY

Paul Callaghan

MERCIER PRESS
IRISH PUBLISHER – IRISH STORY

D1078699

I want to dedicate this, my first cookbook, to my father Michael Callaghan, who passed away in October 1997.

MERCIER PRESS
Cork
www.mercierpress.ie

© Paul Callaghan, 2014

ISBN: 978 1 78117 178 3

10 9 8 7 6 5 4 3 2 1

Printed and bound in the EU.

CONTENTS

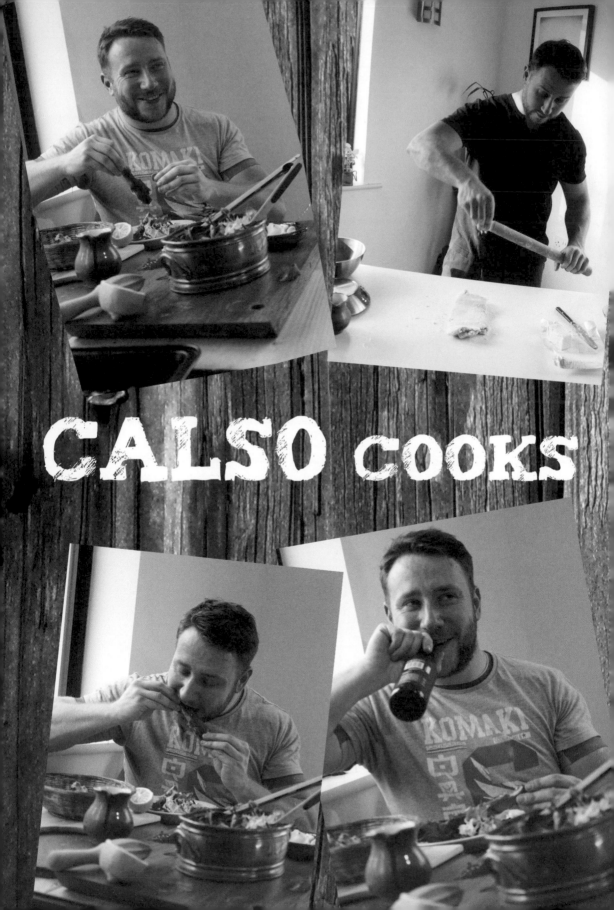

CALSO COOKS

INTRODUCTION

I grew up in a small parish called Derrynoose in County Armagh, Northern Ireland. Derrynoose is a small place with a church, pub, shop and school at the heart of it. It also has its Gaelic football pitch and club, which I was part of while growing up. I wasn't what you would call 'very good' at football, but I did give it a good rattle, playing in goal for a number of years — growing up with three older brothers would accustom you to that role. Throughout my childhood I also dabbled in a little bit of cooking, like most children, helping out my mother with baking apple tarts and the like, but there was nothing to indicate I was 'passionate' about food from an early age. Not surprisingly, I spent most of my time in the kitchen getting in the way, and caused more flour to fall on the floor than into the mixing bowl.

I come from a large family; I am the youngest of nine, with three brothers and five sisters. So my parents made dinners with the intention of stretching their ingredients to the maximum and feeding the troops, rather than tantalising the taste buds. Now please don't get me wrong, I am by no means complaining about the lack of top-notch cooking in the house because I was a fussy wee fella when it came to food. I didn't like vegetables apart from potatoes and I didn't eat lamb or beef. No, my main diet consisted of the trusty spud with lashings of ketchup or beans with either chicken or a pork chop. Can you imagine, after eight agreeable kids, getting landed with a fussy bugger that doesn't eat his veg?!

As I grew up, eating was just one of those things that needed to be done, along with breathing, sleeping, going to Mass and ... well, I would say doing homework, but anyone who knows me knows that I never partook in that exercise at all! I never did quite see the point of homework, I mean, did I not do enough during the day in class? It turns out that no, no I didn't do enough at school! I did, however, ditch CDT (craft, design and technology) for Home Economics ... there was no contest really.

I went on to become a labourer on a plastering squad and then to being a plasterer and having my own successful business — until the building trade went belly up in 2008. So, for a change of scenery and a new start, I decided to make the move to County Clare, as I have a sister married and living down here and I was used to the area from visiting. One thing I was not expecting was to fall madly in love with food, and not just eating it, but growing it, cooking it and everything that goes with it.

When I first moved down to County Clare I was unemployed, trying to start up as a handyman, but I was only getting some small jobs and they were few and far between. I had debts from the loss of my plastering business and it seemed the more I was at home without work and an income, the more the bills and letters demanding money came through the post. I very quickly and very easily fell into depression. The letters would come in and they would be slung unopened into a bottom drawer; the phone calls would be ignored or hung up on. Soon I had no interest in going to do some of the small jobs that did come up. It was a horrible time: worry, stress, mood swings and being generally pissed off with the world. For about eighteen months I lived this way, all the while putting on a front to everyone who knew me and everyone I met.

I rented a small flat for a while, but all I wanted was a house with a bit of space where I could start a small kitchen garden — something that I knew relatively little about, but I still knew it was something I wanted to do from watching TV shows like *River Cottage* and *Jimmy's Farm*. Then the opportunity came up for the house I rent now and I grabbed it with both hands. It has a huge garden and my landlord gave me the go-ahead to make a small kitchen garden, even though he seemed a bit sceptical, probably thinking I would dig a patch then leave it to run wild. But, in growing my own vegetables in the garden, I found a purpose again: this was something to get out of bed for and it gave me a whole new lease of life. In the meantime, since I had moved down, my sister Louise, who is a fantastic cook, had been cooking meals for me with flavours of herbs and spices that I had never experienced before. I can tell you, I was smitten. So I gradually started growing herbs and buying spices, along with different oils, sauces, vinegars etc. and experimenting in cooking and baking with the aid of cookbooks from the local library (I must say that libraries are *the* most fantastic but somehow unused resource around) and advice from my sister.

Cooking became exciting. I couldn't wait to get cooking my next meal and found a hidden passion for cooking for others, waiting to see what they thought of flavour combinations. I started to realise what flavours paired well with each other and how I could introduce herbs and spices into everyday meals to make them more flavoursome. With the fresh produce from my ever-expanding garden and other local fresh produce I just couldn't, and still can't, get enough of experimenting and perfecting recipes in my kitchen. At the start it was probably a terrifying experience coming around for dinner to my house: my guests would be subjected to hearing exactly what every ingredient was and were then force fed as I glared from across the table awaiting any kind of reaction and willing them to 'LIKE IT, GOD DAMN IT' ... but I have toned it down a bit now ... I think!

Over the new year of 2010–11 my eldest sister, Michele, was down visiting and while I was cooking away she suggested I should write down my recipes and maybe even put them online. Throughout January I played with the idea in my head and wondered about creating a website. In February and early March I started typing out all the recipes that I had cooked, with slow, painful, one-fingered typing skills, and I realised I had over eighty recipes. The cost of starting a website was way over my budget, but then I learned about blogging for free. I had always thought 'bloggers' were nerds — it turns out I was right, we are! This was all completely new to me. I bought a relatively good camera and started taking pictures of the dishes I had perfected for myself.

So on 16 March 2011 I set up my blog — www.thesustainablelarder.blogspot.com — and called it 'Calso Cooks from the Sustainable Larder' — Calso being a nickname I had whilst playing football for the mighty 'Noose. Apart from the recipes, I created pages for tips on cooking, herbs and spices, along with a few pages on how to 'grow your own', which I am also very passionate about. It wasn't long before I started building an audience and through the powers of social media I was able to get regular updates out there and share my kind of cooking style with (literally) the world. Since then I have continued growing my own in an ever-expanding vegetable plot, cooking, baking and experimenting in the kitchen and sharing this online on a regular basis. Some of the recipes in the book are from my blog but many of them are new.

The idea for this book came about because not everyone has Internet access and, even if they do, a book is a lot handier to have beside you in the kitchen when following a recipe. And, let's face it, there is nothing like having a cookbook to hand. In addition to this, about two years ago I had a crazy idea: a dream to one day have my own cookbook for sale in shops throughout Ireland, to become a published author. Ninety per cent of me thought that it was just a crazy idea and that 'I wouldn't be good enough to do something like that.' However, I'm happy to say that the other ten per cent drove me on to keep plugging away at the blog and to create an opportunity where one day I might be able to see my cookbook on other people's bookshelves. That other ten per cent said, 'Why not me? I am good enough.' And now, here we are.

If we do not follow our dreams then they are not dreams, only thoughts.

www.thesustainablelarder.com

A HEALTHY, BALANCED DIET

The word diet pisses me off! This is probably because I have tried my fair share — I have always struggled to keep weight off and trying different diets meant that I might lose some weight here and there, but it was always with negative consequences. Cut out the carbs and I was tired, grumpy and felt like shit. Then I went onto the system where you count up your food 'points' — that was good for a while, but then I wanted to live normally again without counting points and the weight went back on within weeks. Then there was the 'I couldn't give a damn' diet! It consisted of drinking wine most nights and gorging on comfort food. That went well until I grew out of all my clothes — something I hadn't done since I was sixteen, except this time I wasn't growing up, I was growing out!

So at that stage I realised I had to do something: the only diet that had ever made sense to me, a diet that has been around for thousands of years, was the Healthy, Balanced Diet. The last time I checked, the word 'diet' in the dictionary is defined as this — 'the food and drink that a person or animal regularly consumes'. Nothing about Atkins, nothing about counting points, nothing about cutting out a main food group. So that is why I am now living my life according to a healthy, balanced diet.

At the end of the day, what we eat and drink determines our state of being. Food and nutrition are crucial to health, not only for the body, but also for the mind and the emotions. Many ailments, sicknesses and diseases can be caused by an unbalanced diet — junk food, takeaways, preservatives, additives, too much salt, sugar and animal fat, too much alcohol and, of course, tobacco — which I know doesn't come into food consumption, but it does suppress hunger and does get in the way of a healthy, balanced diet. Now I'm not preaching off the top of my head: all of the above, with the exception of smoking, used to be a part of my life — I literally am speaking from experience.

Changing my eating habits was the best decision I have ever made — no downside, no repercussions, no negatives. It has led to a healthier body, weight loss (in a healthy way), a healthier mind and a much happier Paul. The way I see it is this: if you have a car — and most of us do — well, that car won't function properly if you don't put the right stuff into it. How far would your car go without the right fuel (carbohydrates), the right oil (protein), the right brake/clutch fluid and power steering oil (fats) and the right coolant (water)? Now I'm certainly no mechanic, but I do know that without the correct type and the correct amounts of all of these you will not have a fully functioning car. The only difference is that a car needs to be serviced once or twice a year — our bodies need to be serviced on a daily basis — a few times a day in fact.

The modern diet has us eating things that are convenient, (unnaturally) colourful and perfectly shaped. Why? Because that's the way society says and thinks it should be. Society needs a good kick up the arse! Walk into a supermarket and take a look at the vegetables on sale: they are all evenly sized, evenly shaped, evenly coloured — now go to a farmers' market or grow your own to know that this is not the way they should be. We are being fed bullshit ... figuratively of course!

So what if a carrot is bent and has a side shoot? So what if peas are not all the same size? So what if some courgettes are plumper at the bottom than the top? It is nature and nature is natural. They all taste great: trust me — I plant, grow, harvest and eat them. Also the 'fresh food' that most supermarkets sell is often sterilised, as it is imported when it's out of season here. They sterilise the food in order to make it 'safe' and to prolong its shelf-life whilst in the store. This sterilisation kills the bad bacteria that would make the food go bad, but it also kills the good bacteria that are vital for a healthy digestive system, so that food is quite simply lifeless and of much less benefit to you. What I would suggest is, if you cannot grow your own fresh food, then buy at farmers' markets or as local as possible where you can.

A healthy, balanced diet has been around for thousands of years — it is not a new fad. The mainstay of a healthy diet should be carbohydrates and fibre. Foods like potatoes, lentils, wholewheat pasta, wholegrain bread, brown rice and cereals provide this. To these, protein-based foods like meat, fish, eggs or beans should be added in smaller amounts. It is not necessary to have meat or fish with every meal — not even every day. The other ingredients to be added for a healthy diet are essential fatty acids from nuts, seeds, oils and oily fish. And this, along with vitamins, minerals and phytochemicals found naturally in fruit and vegetables, is the basic template for healthy eating.

History tells us that this healthy template has been used worldwide in all cultures. Civilisations throughout history relied on this combination: in America they used corn and beans as their staple diet; in Asia it was/is rice and soy; in Africa wheat, millet, chickpeas or beans; in Europe wheat, rye, barley, oats, beans and pulses like lentils. They were traditionally used with a variety of fruit and vegetables (mostly raw), along with fish and meat when available. Then fermented foods like yogurt, curd, pickled vegetables, beer, cider and wine, all of which have beneficial properties for the intestine, were added through the ages. The diet is rich in friendly bacteria, fibre and nutrients, and helps balance and maintain a healthy intestine; it is a diet which is ideally suited to the human body.

For me, maintaining a healthy lifestyle is or should be common sense, of which having a healthy diet and watching what you eat is only a part. You can be getting the percentages right — carbs versus protein versus fats — and you can be eating very fresh produce too, but if you don't watch portion sizes and don't get up off your backside and do some exercise, then you will find that a healthy, balanced diet may not make you look and feel as good as it should. There is no point in me going into depth on portion sizes as everyone's size, metabolism rate and daily exercise routine is different ... it wouldn't be very accurate. Common sense goes a long way, but if you are really stuck then a dietician would be happy to create a plan for portion sizes taking everything into account.

5 key steps to a healthier diet:

Cut down on convenience food and takeaways.

Try replacing meat with oily fish more often.

Reduce your intake of sugar, salt, coffee, fizzy drinks and alcohol.

Make your diet as varied as possible.

Use fresh ingredients as often as possible.

I fully understand that all this is not possible for everyone, but if we try and make even small changes to our eating habits, we will all benefit from it. Use the 'bads' in moderation and the 'goods' as much as possible.

GOOD FATS v. BAD FATS

When it comes to losing weight, people automatically think that they must cut out all fats. This is simply not true: there are four types of fats, two of which are good and two that are bad. Your body needs the good fats in the same way it needs carbs and proteins — that's why most people will talk about a 'balanced diet'.

A balanced diet consists roughly of 55% carbohydrates, 15% protein and 30% fats. The carbs give us the energy we need for day-to-day tasks, the protein gives us the recovery we need in our muscles (every movement you make uses some muscles, so this is not just for those who work out) and the fats are another source of energy and are needed to extract nutrients from the foods we eat.

It is a myth that all fats are equal and equally bad. The fact is that Saturated Fats and Trans Fats are bad for you: they raise cholesterol and increase the risk of heart disease. Monounsaturated Fats and Polyunsaturated Fats do the opposite: they lower cholesterol and decrease the risk of heart disease. DO NOT cut out fats altogether — the key to a healthy diet is to swap more bad fats for good.

GOOD FATS

Monounsaturated fats: certain nuts (almonds, peanuts, cashews, hazelnuts, peanut butter), olive oil, peanut oil, sesame oil, avocados, olives.

Polyunsaturated fats: oily fish (tuna, salmon, trout, sardines, mackerel), seeds (sunflower, sunflower oil, pumpkin, flaxseed), soymilk and tofu.

BAD FATS

Saturated Fats: high fat cuts of beef, pork, lamb; chicken skin; whole-fat milk and yogurt; butter; cheese; ice cream.

Trans Fats: commercially baked cookies, doughnuts and pastries (there are far more ingredients and preservatives in commercially baked goods than those you make at home); packaged snack food like microwave popcorn, crisps, biscuits, crackers and chocolate bars; fried foods: chips, chicken, chicken nuggets etc.

So we can make the change by replacing the bad fats with the good, limit our fast-food intake, avoid commercially baked goods and limit our saturated fats.

Other ideas are to bake or grill instead of frying or deep-frying, trim excess fat off meat, remove the skin from chicken, choose low-fat milk and cheese.

Now while my recipes do include some of these 'bad fats' they are quite limited. Besides, one small 'bad' ingredient in a meal won't make the meal unhealthy, in the same way that a piece of lettuce and a slice of tomato won't make a Big-Mac meal healthy ... now you know that makes sense!

HERBS AND SPICES

Both herbs and spices are quite inexpensive and really are worth using in every-day cooking for both flavour and health purposes.

Growing your own herbs couldn't be easier: they can be grown in a small bed, in patio tubs or window boxes, inside or outside. One packet of seeds that cost about €2 will keep you in herbs for a full year — or up to five years for some herbs like thyme, sage and rosemary. Alternatively, they are easy to buy in garden centres and in most supermarkets as plants, fresh cuts or dried herbs.

You can pick up a small jar of spice (normally about 40–50g) for around €1.50 and this will last you 1–2 months, if not longer. I use spices in almost everything I cook and I have never found myself going to the supermarket to look for more than one jar at a time.

I have always believed nature has a remedy for everything, but on doing my research on the health benefits of various foods, I was blown away with just how beneficial herbs and spices are to your body. They are packed full of antioxidants and all the vitamins you need to make your body a fortress against disease, bacteria and bugs. So, not only do herbs and spices make cooking and eating a more fun and tasty experience, they kick ass too!

ESSENTIAL KITCHEN HERBS

BASIL

Add chopped stalks to cooking and add the leaves at the last minute of cooking. It is great in salads and as a garnish. Basil flavours Mediterranean vegetables really well. It pairs well with cheese, courgettes, eggs, garlic, lemons, olives, peas, pine nuts, pizza, potatoes, raspberries, rice, sweetcorn and tomatoes.

Basil has anti-inflammatory properties, it is packed full of antioxidants and aids your defences against asthma and arthritis.

BAY LEAF

Add to soups, stews and sauces. Also use for marinades, pickles and roasting dishes. Always remove before serving. It pairs well with citrus flavours, fish, game, lentils, meat, onions, poultry, root vegetables and tomatoes.

Bay can balance blood sugar levels and it retards weight gain. It can also reduce high blood pressure.

CHERVIL

Best used as a garnish due to its mild flavour: sprinkle over soups and salads. It can also be put in omelettes at the last minute. It pairs well with asparagus, beans, beetroot, carrots, cream cheese, eggs, fennel, peas, potatoes, poultry, tomatoes, mushrooms and seafood.

Chervil can relieve fluid retention, lower blood pressure and is rich in vitamins A and C.

CHIVES

If adding to your cooking, always add them at the end, as their flavour will fizzle out if cooked too much. They can be eaten raw in salads, sauces and in soups as a garnish. They are part of the onion family so have a delicate onion flavour. They pair well with avocados, courgettes, cream cheese, eggs, fish, potatoes, root vegetables and seafood.

Studies are showing that chives may reduce the risk of prostate cancer.

CORIANDER LEAVES

Coriander leaves can be cooked in curries, stir-fries and soups, or used in pesto, salads and chutneys. They are also used for garnishing. Coriander pairs well with avocados, chillies, cucumber, coconut, fish, meat, onion, poultry, rice, root vegetables, seafood and squashes.

Coriander is effective against high cholesterol levels, stomach ulcers, anaemia, digestion disorders, conjunctivitis and skin disorders. It is rich in antioxidants and contains vitamins A and C.

DILL

Add dill at the end of cooking and as a garnish to salads and fish dishes. It pairs well with beetroot, beans, carrots, celeriac, cucumber, eggs, fish, potatoes, seafood and spinach.

Dill can help the growth of good bacteria in the body.

FENNEL

Fennel gives a liquorice flavour to soups and chowders, and roast meat and fish dishes. It pairs well with beetroot, beans, cabbage, duck, fish, leeks, pork, potatoes, rice, seafood and tomatoes.

Fennel can relieve congestion, stomach cramps and headaches.

MARJORAM

Not unlike oregano, but milder in flavour and a little sweeter. Use the leaves in salads, cream sauces, scrambled eggs or omelettes and in fish dishes. Pairs well with eggs, fish, mushrooms and squashes.

Marjoram contains antioxidants and has anti-bacterial properties.

MINT

Used in sweet and savoury dishes and also in drinks, for flavour and garnishing. It pairs well with carrots, chocolate, cucumber, curries, duck, lamb, lime, potatoes and yogurt.

Mint aids digestion, heartburn and irritable bowel syndrome. It eases and unblocks respiratory passageways and can relieve the effects of colds and nasal allergies. It also has calming properties and is a good blood cleanser.

OREGANO

Great for flavouring fish dishes, vegetable dishes, pizzas and lasagnes. Often very effective when used dried. Pairs well with beef, coriander, cheeses, chicken, chillies, cumin, garlic, lamb, pork and squashes.

Oregano has four times the antioxidants that the 'superfood' blueberries have and it kills unfriendly bacteria.

PARSLEY

Use flat leaf parsley for garnishing and add it chopped to sauces. Curly leaf parsley can be used for soups and stews, stalks and all. It pairs well with chicken, eggs, fish, garlic, lemons, lentils, onions, rice, seafood and tomatoes.

Parsley is a good source of antioxidants and 'heart healthy' nutrients. It also contains vitamins A and C.

ROSEMARY

Can be eaten finely chopped in soups, stews and casseroles; also good in meat, poultry and roast vegetable dishes and used in marinades. Put a whole sprig in to flavour roast dishes. The woody sprigs when stripped of their leaves can be used as flavoursome skewers for kebabs. It pairs well with beef, cabbage, chillies, courgettes, eggs, fish, all game, lamb, lemons, lentils, onions, peppers, pork, poultry, potatoes and squashes.

Rosemary contains antioxidants that stop the gene mutations that lead to cancer and it may help treat damage to blood vessels to reduce the risk of heart attack.

SAGE

Quite a strong herb so use sparingly to avoid overpowering other flavours. Great with roast dishes and used in stuffings and marinades. It pairs well with apples, beans, bay leaf, celery, chicken, duck, game, garlic, liver, onions, pork and tomatoes.

Sage aids digestion of oily and fatty foods. It also contains antioxidants, has anti-inflammatory properties and is known to improve brain function.

TARRAGON

Again, use sparingly as it is quite strong in flavour. Great for flavouring fish dishes, chicken and game. Pairs well with asparagus, cheese, chicken, courgettes, eggs, fish, game, mushrooms, potatoes, seafood and tomatoes.

Tarragon is packed full of antioxidants and has antifungal properties.

THYME

Use in stews, casseroles, marinades and terrines; it is great in roast dishes like chicken, beef, game and vegetables. Pairs well with carrots, chicken, duck, fish, lamb, onions, potatoes, rabbit, sweetcorn, tomatoes, turkey and wild mushrooms.

Thyme helps digestion of oily and fatty foods. It is packed with antioxidants and can kill MRSA infections.

ESSENTIAL KITCHEN SPICES

ALLSPICE

Allspice has long been used for preserving meats and fish. It is a good general spice that will lift any dish; great for adding into curries for extra flavour. It pairs well with onion, root vegetables, squashes, tomatoes, white cabbage and most fruit.

Allspice can help balance blood sugar levels.

CARAWAY SEEDS

These little beauties are used for flavouring in rye bread. They go wonderfully in stews, as well as in beef and vegetable dishes. They pair well with apples, beef, bread, cabbage, duck, goose, pork, potatoes, root vegetables and tomatoes.

These little seeds are a rich source of dietary fibre.

CARDAMOM PODS

Lightly bruise and fry the pods and add directly to rice, but remove before serving, or grind the seeds and add to pastries, puddings, breads, etc. They pair well with apples, cinnamon, cloves, oranges, pears, pulses, star anise and sweet potatoes.

They reduce stomach acid that leads to heartburn and they aid the digestion of grains.

CAYENNE PEPPER

Sharp, warm and fiery, less is more in this case to prevent overpowering a dish. Cayenne pepper is chilli flakes ground very finely. It pairs well with chicken, eggs, fish and potatoes.

Contains capsaicin, which is an anti-inflammatory that helps to relieve pain, eases congestion and clears mucus from the lungs and nose. It also assists in weight loss and helps boost immunity.

CHILLI FLAKES

Add dried chilli flakes to fire up any dish. They pair well with most savoury ingredients and with chocolate.

Contains capsaicin (see cayenne pepper above).

CINNAMON

A great all round spice used in sweet and savoury dishes, also used in hot drinks like coffee, tea, hot chocolate and mulled wine. It pairs well with almonds, apples, apricots, banana, chocolate, coffee, lamb, pears, red cabbage and rice.

Cinnamon can stop the growth of bacteria, fungus and yeast. It has anti-clotting and anti-inflammatory properties. It is also a rich source of antioxidants and boosts brain function.

CLOVES

Mostly used ground with rich meats, also used in pies and cakes, syrups and pre-serves. They pair well with beetroot, carrots, chocolate, cinnamon, duck, fruits, ham, onions, oranges and venison.

Cloves are an effective painkiller and can alleviate diarrhoea and nausea.

CORIANDER SEEDS

Use ground up in vegetable dishes, stews and curries. Also used whole in marinades and pickles. They pair well with chicken, citrus, cumin, fish, ham, mushrooms, onions, pork and potatoes.

Coriander seeds are anti-inflammatory, reduce cholesterol and alleviate stom-ach cramps and chronic gout.

CUMIN SEEDS

Use the whole seeds or ground seeds in soups, stews, casseroles and curries. Dry toast the seeds in a frying pan to release more aroma before crushing in a pestle and mortar. They pair well with coriander, cheese, chilli, meats, oregano, poultry and vegetables.

Cumin seeds can be a memory enhancer and work as an anti-inflammatory.

CURRY LEAVES

Use in long-simmered curries to extract their flavour, then remove before serving. They pair well with cardamom seeds, chilli, coconut, coriander, cumin, fish, garlic, lamb, rice, seafood and vegetables.

Curry leaves can aid digestive problems and are used in India for severe nausea during pregnancy.

GINGER

A firm favourite with me! Use grated or finely diced in stir-fries, soups, sauces and marinades. Also used in chutneys, relishes and rice dishes. Use ground ginger for baking in cakes, biscuits and in desserts. It pairs well with chilli, citrus, coconut, fish, garlic, meat, most vegetables, orchard fruits, poultry, rhubarb, seafood and soy.

Ginger helps with nausea, vomiting, motion sickness and morning sickness. It is a powerful antioxidant and is also a common digestive aid for the side effects of chemotherapy.

NUTMEG

A wonderful spice used in both sweet and savoury dishes, from mashed potatoes, stews and casseroles to milk puddings and fruit desserts. It is best to use whole nutmeg and grate it fresh with a micro-grater rather than buying it ground. It pairs well with cardamom, cheese, chicken, couscous, eggs, lamb, milk, onions, potatoes, root vegetables, spinach and squashes.

This woody nut kills cavity-causing bacteria in the mouth, relaxes muscles and can help combat asthma.

ONION SEEDS

Also known as Nigella seeds. Add to curries and pickles or sprinkle seeds on breads and savoury pasties before baking. They pair well with allspice, coriander, cumin, potatoes, rice, root vegetables and star anise.

Onion seeds help reduce blood pressure and can be used to relieve the symptoms of the common cold.

PAPRIKA

Can be sweet, hot or smoked. Use sweet or hot varieties in soups, tagines and as a garnish. Use smoked paprika as a rub. Pairs well with most meats and vegetables as well as with eggs, fish and onions.

Contains capsaicin, which is an anti-inflammatory that helps to relieve pain, ease congestion and clears mucus from the lungs and nose. It also assists in weight loss and helps boost immunity.

PEPPERCORNS

Black peppercorns can be used whole to flavour liquids like stock and marinades, or used freshly ground for everything else. White peppercorns can be used in clear or pale sauces. They pair well with fish, game, herbs, oils, meats, salt and seafood.

Peppercorns improve digestion and they promote digestive health. They stimulate the breakdown of fat cells and are powerful antioxidants with anti-bacterial and anti-inflammatory properties.

SAFFRON

Used in fish soups and stews, also in risottos, paellas and in baking. Infuse the strands and add in early to enrich the colour or add in later for a stronger flavour. Part of the crocus flower, it is more expensive by the gram than gold! It pairs well with asparagus, chicken, eggs, fish, game, leeks, mayonnaise, seafood, spinach and squash.

It is rich in antioxidants and vitamins A and C.

STAR ANISE

Used in Chinese and Vietnamese cooking, this works well in fish and seafood dishes as well as when poaching fruit and making mulled wine. It pairs well with chicken, cinnamon, chilli, coriander, fennel, figs, fish, garlic, ginger, leeks, meats, pears, root vegetables, seafood and tropical fruits.

Star anise is a natural diuretic.

VANILLA PODS

Use whole or split to flavour poached fruit, sugar, milk and desserts. Scrape out the seeds for creams, custards and ice cream. Also use pure vanilla extract (liquid) or vanilla paste in baking. Pairs well with apples, chocolate, cream, milk, rhubarb, seafood, strawberries and sugar.

Vanilla contains small amounts of both vitamin B and iron.

GROWING
YOUR OWN

Now I am not going to go into details here as quite simply, I could write a whole book on the topic — and I will one day! It is something I love doing and really encourage others to do too. Growing your own fruit and vegetables has never been easier or, in my opinion, more needed. All shop-bought fruit and vegetables unfortunately come with a price: either the regular stuff has been screwed around with — forced, sprayed with chemicals and/or been kept in cold storage for God knows how long — or the organic stuff comes with a hefty price tag.

If you have some garden space I would highly recommend giving some time and effort to preparing the ground or building some low-cost raised beds so you can try your hand at sowing, growing and harvesting your own crops. This can be as big or as small as you wish, from a few herbs or some salad veggies, to rows of potatoes, cabbages, carrots and the like. If you are stuck for space then most fruit and veg can be grown very successfully in containers like patio tubs and window boxes ... so no excuses! And if, like me, you start small and slowly build, then it ensures you don't become overwhelmed with the task at hand and it gives you plenty of time to plan ahead and learn by doing.

Growing your own has become popular again and rightly so — at least you know exactly what you are eating, how it has been grown and how it has been treated. Every garden centre in the country has all the supplies you need to start your own kitchen garden and even most supermarkets are selling seeds.

When I first started out I had no idea what I was doing but, with the help of the Internet and some library books, I taught myself everything I needed to know. It hasn't been without its challenges and failures, but that is all part of the learning experience. Plus, it got me out of the house and gave me a whole new lease of life — I would definitely recommend it for those who are feeling stuck in a rut like I was. Just watching nature at its best gives you a wonderful feeling, not to mention the health benefits of eating your own crops on a daily/ weekly basis.

Growing your own is a wonderful thing to introduce to your children, great for them to get involved with and ultimately to get them eating a fresh supply of what you produce. It is certainly better than dragging them away from their consoles to eat processed rubbish food like chicken nuggets and ready meals.

So go on ... give growing your own a try and you will, quite literally, reap what you sow!

COOKING ESSENTIALS

Store cupboard ingredients are the ingredients we use in everyday cooking, from salt and pepper to stock and oils, from rice and pasta to tinned tomatoes and relishes. Each week while shopping I am gradually adding to, or replenishing my store cupboard ingredients. Without them we would all be at a loss when it comes to making home-made meals.

I know what you may be thinking: 'But I'm on a budget each week, I can't afford to be buying other items that I haven't accounted for.' However, if you invest in good store cupboard ingredients they will save you money in the long term. Some morning you wake up to a hungry household — you don't have bread for toasting or cereal in the press, but you do have a bag of flour, an egg and some milk. Right there you have enough pancake batter to feed those hungry mouths. Or at dinner time, the cupboards are looking bare but you have some dried pasta, a tin of chopped tomatoes, some last few bits of veg and some dried herbs — well there is the basis for a lovely home-made Italian meal. What I am trying to say is that you should re-evaluate your shopping list and realise that home-made will work out cheaper and taste better than the convenient brands out there. I do use shop-bought sauces and convenient products too, but I certainly don't rely on them for every meal. Look: cooking can be as extravagant or as basic as you want, but either way you need the foundations.

All these store cupboard ingredients are the foundations of every good home-cooked meal, and if you keep your larder well stocked with the basics you will never go hungry. It will only be a matter of adding vegetables and/or meat to whizz up a good honest family meal.

IN MY LARDER:

Herbs and spices: see pp. 12–18

Oils: olive oil, rapeseed oil, toasted sesame oil

Vinegar: red wine, white wine, cider, balsamic, malt

Flour, etc.: plain, self-raising, wholemeal, type-00, baking powder

Mustard: Dijon, wholegrain, English

Sauces, etc.: soy sauce, oyster sauce, Worcestershire sauce, honey, maple syrup, Tabasco, pesto

Dried foods: wholemeal pasta sheets/short pasta/spaghetti, couscous, egg noodles, rice noodles, pulses and grains, porridge oats, stock cubes (beef, chicken and vegetable), dried yeast

Tinned/jarred food: chopped tomatoes, green beans, anchovy fillets, redcurrant jelly, horseradish sauce, peanut butter

Sea salt and black pepper

CONVERSION CHARTS

DRY INGREDIENTS

Metric	Imperial
5 grams	⅛ ounce
10g	¼ oz
15g	½ oz
20g	¾ oz
25g	1 oz
50g	2 oz
75g	3 oz
100–125g	4 oz
150g	5 oz
175g	6 oz
200g	7 oz
225g	8 oz
250g	9 oz
275g	10 oz
300g	11 oz
325g	12 oz
350g	13 oz
400g	14 oz
425g	15 oz
450g	1 lb
1kg (1000g)	2¼ lb

SPOON MEASURES

1 teaspoon	5ml
2 teaspoons	10ml
1 tablespoon	15ml
2 tablespoons	30ml
3 tablespoons	45ml
4 tablespoons	60ml
5 tablespoons	75ml

LIQUIDS

Metric	Imperial
25ml	1 floz
50	2
75	3
125	4
150	5
175	6
200	7
225	8
250	9
275	10
500ml	0.87 pint
1 litre (1000ml)	1.75 pints
American cup	8 fluid ounces
Small glass	150ml

OVEN HEAT AND TEMPERATURES

Most electric ovens are multi-purpose and will have a fan-assisted setting and this is what I use. I find it is better to use this setting as it distributes the heat around the oven for more even, faster cooking than a conventional oven. If you use a conventional oven you will need to increase the temperature and the cooking time may be a little longer. It is best to consult your cooker manual for this as ovens will vary, but the table provided gives a general guide to the necessary temperature adjustments, as well as the equivalent Gas Mark and Fahrenheit temperatures.

CELSIUS	FAN	FAHRENHEIT	GAS
140	120	275	1
150	130	300	2
160/170	140/150	325	3
180	160	350	4
190	170	375	5
200	180	400	6
220	200	425	7
230	210	450	8
240	220	475	9

BREAKFAST

AVOCADO, CRISPY BACON AND LIME ON TOAST

FEEDS 4

INGREDIENTS

2 ripe avocados
Juice of 1 lime
Salt and black pepper to season
8 slices of streaky bacon
8 thick slices of rye bread (or similar)
Parsley to garnish

Do yourself a favour and make this recipe. I use this for a breakfast when I can take the time to savour and enjoy it! It is also great for a light lunch. I try and use nice fresh rye bread or a spelt and honey loaf. Butter or margarine on the toast is not necessary as the avocado is nice and moist. Try and get the bacon nice and crispy and the fatty bits slightly charred for maximum flavour.

METHOD

1 Halve, de-stone and slice the avocado into 1cm slices, place in a large bowl and drizzle with the lime juice, season well with salt and pepper, and give them a good toss. Set aside uncovered for 10 minutes.

2 In the meantime grill the streaky bacon until well coloured on both sides and set on kitchen paper to crisp up.

3 Toast the thick bread slices, then arrange the avocado slices on top, add the crispy bacon and lightly spoon over any remaining juice from the bowl.

4 Garnish with parsley and serve immediately.

BAKED EGGS WITH CROISSANTS AND JAM

FEEDS 2

INGREDIENTS

Butter for greasing

2 croissants

Raspberry jam (or your favourite flavour)

3 medium eggs

Splash of milk

1 teaspoon brown sugar

A sprinkle of cinnamon to serve

This may sound like an odd combination but it works. I find breakfasts like these are great for a lazy Sunday morning when you can take your time and enjoy the prospect of a big Sunday roast dinner later. Don't feel like you have to make the croissants either: shop-bought ones are just fine. As much as I love to make most of my meals, I still try and make some things fuss free, hence the above-mentioned 'lazy Sunday morning'.

METHOD

1 Preheat the oven to 180°C. Lightly butter two large ramekins or two small ovenproof dishes and place on a baking tray, as ingredients can spill over.

2 Tear each of the croissants into four or five large pieces and spread jam on each piece, then divide the pieces among the dishes.

3 In a measuring jug (handy for pouring) beat the eggs, then add a splash of milk and the brown sugar and beat again. Pour into the two dishes to just over three-quarters full.

4 Bake in the oven for 30–35 minutes. Sprinkle with some cinnamon to serve.

BANANA AND OAT MUFFINS

Muffins are a great 'smash and grab' breakfast.

They keep well for a few days in an airtight container so they can be made at a time of your convenience and used for those mornings where there is a rush on ... or a snooze button pressed too many times — we've all been there!

MAKES 12

INGREDIENTS

260g self-raising flour

1 teaspoon cinnamon

½ teaspoon baking powder

100g porridge oats

100g soft brown sugar

2 medium eggs

185ml low-fat natural yogurt

60ml rapeseed oil

2 ripe bananas mashed

METHOD

1 Preheat your oven to 200°C. Line a muffin tray with muffin cases.

2 Sift the flour, cinnamon and baking powder into a large mixing bowl. Add the oats and brown sugar.

3 Whisk the eggs in a medium mixing bowl and mix in the yogurt and oil. Add in the mashed bananas and combine well.

4 Add the wet mix to the dry flour mix and combine with a wooden spoon – the mix does not have to be fully smooth.

5 Divide the mix evenly among the muffin cases. Bake in the oven for 25 minutes, or until a skewer inserted in the middle comes out clean. Remove and when cool enough to handle, place on a cooling rack until fully cool.

BEST OF BOTH PANCAKES

MAKES 6–8

By best of both, I mean using half plain flour and half wholemeal flour. This is one of my favourite filling breakfasts, but of course it doesn't just have to be for breakfast — it can be lunch or supper. Pancake batter is best if made a few hours in advance or even the night before; just cover with cling film and leave in the fridge, then whisk it up again before use.

a pancake is not just for Shrove Tuesday ... it's for life!

INGREDIENTS

125g plain flour
125g wholemeal flour
Pinch of salt
500ml skimmed milk
2 medium eggs
Rapeseed oil

METHOD

1 Spoon both flours into a mixing bowl and add the salt. Pour in half the milk and crack the eggs in. Give it all a good whisk and add more milk if required – you're looking for a batter with the consistency of double cream.

2 Pop a pan on a hot hob and add a light drizzle of oil, wait until pan starts to smoke a little and pour some mixture in the centre. Lift the pan and rotate your wrist around, spreading the mixture so that it fills the base of the pan.

3 After a minute, flip it over using a fish slice. Another minute or two and it will be cooked. You only need to flip it once, unless you want to show off!

4 There is no end to what you can serve these with – everyone has their favourites, but for me it is simply butter and sugar.

BREAKFAST PIZZA

MAKES 4

Now you may be thinking, 'What is healthy about a pizza for breakfast?'

Let me explain. Pizza dough is basically bread — the same mix will make a loaf of plain white bread. It is just rolled out and baked differently. For most people it is normal to have grilled or fried sausage, bacon, black or white pudding and mushrooms with eggs for breakfast on a weekend, along with bread (I'm not saying this is healthy option, but a weekly indulgence is no harm!). Well here it is combined in all its glory with a tomato-based sauce and a little cheese. I like this as a treat breakfast or brunch. I normally make it when I have visitors, just so they have something they are not used to seeing and, by God, it never fails to impress! I usually use a boiled egg, sliced, but there is nothing stopping you from frying an egg, then cutting it up and putting it over as a topping, or cracking a few quail's eggs over the top.

INGREDIENTS

1 quantity pizza base (see p. 93)
2–3 sausages
2–3 rashers
4–5 slices of black pudding
4–5 mushrooms
4 tablespoons tomato-based
   pasta sauce – shop-bought or
   home-made
1–2 boiled eggs
Cheddar cheese

METHOD

1 Make the pizza dough according to the instructions on page 93. Preheat the oven to the maximum temperature (usually around 250°C).

2 Take a ball of pizza dough a little smaller than a tennis ball and roll it out as thinly as possible – don't worry about making a perfect circle.

3 Part-grill the sausages, rashers and black pudding and cut up into bite-sized pieces. Slice the mushrooms. Pop the pizza base onto an oiled pizza tray and spread a tablespoon of pasta sauce over it. Grate a small amount of cheese of your choice over the top (I just use low-fat cheddar), then add all the toppings.

4 Bake for 15–20 minutes for a lovely crispy breakfast pizza.

TIP: You can freeze the egg yolks and use them in other recipes.

CHERRY TOMATO AND HERB HEART-HEALTHY OMELETTE

FEEDS 1

INGREDIENTS

4–6 cherry tomatoes
Olive oil
Sea salt and black pepper to season
1 large egg, plus 3 egg whites
A handful of chopped mixed herbs of
   your choice
Cheddar cheese (optional)

This is mainly an egg white omelette, although you can of course make a regular one including the egg yolks. However, once you give this a try you will see that it is just as good without the yolks and much better for your heart. I add in one yolk just for colour. The sweetness of the cherry tomatoes really comes through to meet the sharp herbs. I normally use herbs like chives, flat leaf parsley or mint — or a mix of them all.

METHOD

1 Halve or quarter the cherry tomatoes, pour some oil into a non-stick pan and tip the tomatoes in. Season them well and fry them off for 1–2 minutes until just soft.

2 In the meantime put the grill onto a high heat. Separate the eggs, then lightly beat the whites and one yolk in a bowl.

3 Scatter the chopped herbs over the tomatoes and pour the beaten eggs over.

4 Quickly stir the eggs with a silicon spatula to spread them out and make sure they cook evenly. Take off the heat as they start to set, grate a little cheese over the top (if using) and place under the grill for 2–3 minutes. Slide onto a warm plate and serve immediately.

MELON AND YOGURT CRUNCH POTS

These are a super healthy, fast and delicious start to the day … and not a cooker in sight.

INGREDIENTS

1 melon or a melon medley pack
Natural low-fat yogurt
A handful of bran cereal
A handful of sunflower seeds
A small handful of raisins
Honey

FEEDS 4

METHOD

1 Chop the melon into roughly bite-sized pieces.

2 Divide them among four tumblers, pour some yogurt over the top, top this with the cereal, sunflower seeds and raisins, and finish off with a squirt of honey. Serve immediately.

OATS-SO-PEACHY BREAKFAST BAKE

This is definitely a treat breakfast, but if you can't spoil yourself in the morning when can you? It's also very high in fibre and vitamins, *so it's not all bad!*

INGREDIENTS

120g porridge oats
55g brown sugar
Pinch of salt
1 teaspoon baking powder
2 egg whites
125ml skimmed milk
1 teaspoon rapeseed oil
1 teaspoon vanilla extract
1 tin of peaches – drained
A small handful of dried cranberries
A small handful of raisins
Oil for greasing
2 teaspoons chopped walnuts

METHOD

1 Preheat the oven to 180°C.

2 In a medium bowl mix the oats, sugar, salt and baking powder. In another medium bowl gently whisk the egg whites, milk, oil and vanilla extract.

3 Pour the wet mixture into the dry ingredients in the first bowl and give it all a stir. Allow to sit for about 5–7 minutes until the oats have absorbed all the liquid.

4 Chop the peaches roughly and stir them into the mix along with the cranberries and raisins.

5 Lightly oil a medium-sized oven dish or four individual-portion-sized oven-proof dishes and divide the mixture between them.

6 Top with a sprinkle of chopped walnuts and bake for 30–35 minutes.

7 Allow to stand for 5 minutes when it is finished cooking, then serve up with some low-fat natural yogurt.

PINEAPPLE AND MINT FRAPPÉ

FEEDS 4

A 'frappé' is a fruit-flavoured ice drink. I have this in the breakfast section, as it is **a wonderful way to start the day,** but it can also make a great summer's evening drink while sitting out in the sun and can be livened up with a dash of a spirit (of your choice) to make a cocktail — not recommended for mornings!

INGREDIENTS

1 pineapple
8–12 fresh mint leaves
12–14 ice cubes
A squirt of honey
Mint leaves to serve

METHOD

1 Top and tail the pineapple, then carefully shave off the sides and cut into chunks. Wash the mint leaves.

2 Place the pineapple, the mint leaves, ice and a squirt of honey into a good blender and blitz until silky smooth.

3 Divide among four glasses.

PUMPKIN SEED SCONES

Scones can be plain or have dried fruit in them, like raisins or sultanas, but I like to put seeds in mine, or a mix of seeds and fruit. There is nothing like making a fresh batch of scones first thing in the morning, the only problem being that I find it hard to stop eating until they are gone!

MAKES 12

INGREDIENTS

450g plain flour, plus some for dusting
2 teaspoons baking powder
A pinch of salt
115g butter
60g sugar
A handful of pumpkin seeds
275ml skimmed milk
1 medium egg

METHOD

1 Preheat the oven to 180°C.

2 Put the flour, baking powder and salt into a large mixing bowl (no need to sift), add the butter and rub it into the flour using your fingertips until lump free and well incorporated. Stir in the sugar and pumpkin seeds with a wooden spoon.

3 Beat the milk and egg together in a jug.

4 Make a well in the middle of the dry ingredients in the bowl and pour most of the milk and beaten egg in (reserve a little to glaze the scones) and fold this all together until it forms a dough.

5 Dust a clean work surface with flour and scrape the dough out onto it. Dust the dough with more flour and gently knead it into a ball. Roll it out until it is about an inch thick and cut out in circles using a pastry cutter (use up all the dough by reforming and rolling).

6 Place the circles on two greased and floured flat baking trays and use a pastry brush to glaze the tops with the reserved milk and egg mix.

7 Place in the preheated oven for 25–30 minutes until risen and lightly golden, then transfer to a wire rack to cool.

RUSTIC BACON, EGG AND CHEESE PIE

This is a very simple breakfast/brunch.

I would normally serve this up to visitors as a no fuss brunch. As long as you remember to thaw your pastry the night before, this can be prepared and cooked in no time.

FEEDS
4–6

INGREDIENTS

250g packet of puff pastry
150g sour cream
20g low-fat cheddar cheese, grated
1 whole medium egg, plus 2 egg yolks
2–3 rashers of uncooked bacon, chopped
2 teaspoons fresh thyme leaves
Milk for glazing
Salad leaves and balsamic dressing to serve

METHOD

1 Preheat the oven to 180°C.

2 Roll out the pastry on a clean, lightly floured work surface and shape it to fit a 33cm/13in x 23cm/9in baking tray.

3 Line the tray with baking paper and lay the pastry on top.

4 Whisk together the sour cream, cheese and eggs in a large bowl and stir in the bacon and thyme leaves. Carefully pour this into the centre of the pastry, leaving a 2½ cm/1in border of pastry around the edge.

5 Brush the border with the milk using a pastry brush. Bake for 15 minutes until the pastry border has risen and is golden.

6 Serve hot.

SPICED FRENCH TOAST WITH WALNUTS, BLUEBERRIES AND MAPLE SYRUP

Growing up, French toast was something I had for supper, but now it's a regular breakfast feature.

INGREDIENTS

2 medium eggs
40ml skimmed milk
1 tablespoon brown sugar
A sprinkle of cinnamon
A small handful of walnuts, coarsely chopped
Rapeseed oil
4 slices of good wholegrain bread
100g blueberries – fresh or frozen ones that have been thawed
Maple syrup (optional)

FEEDS 2

METHOD

1 In a large mixing bowl lightly whisk together the eggs, milk, sugar and cinnamon, then set aside.

2 Heat a non-stick pan on a medium heat and toast the walnuts for a few minutes, then set these aside in a spare bowl.

3 Add a splash of rapeseed oil to the pan and increase the heat to high. Dip both sides of a slice of the bread into the egg mixture, letting it soak in well. Cook in the hot pan for 1–2 minutes on either side and repeat this for the four slices, keeping them warm when cooked in a medium heated oven.

4 Serve the French toast with the chopped walnuts, blueberries and a generous drizzle of maple syrup.

SUPER SMOOTHIES

I think that Smoothies make a great breakfast; they can be really healthy (depending on the ingredients!) and super quick to make if you are in a rush in the mornings. There are so many combinations you can try and, as always, experimentation is key — let yourself go, live a little! These are four of my favourites:

BREAKFAST OF CHAMPIONS

This has a great balance of carbs, protein and good fats to kick-start your day.

INGREDIENTS

400ml skimmed milk

1 ripe banana

30g porridge oats

1 tablespoon drinking chocolate powder

1 tablespoon peanut butter

1 tablespoon honey

METHOD

Blend until smooth.

CRANBERRY AND RASPBERRY SMOOTHIE

INGREDIENTS

200ml cranberry juice

100ml skimmed milk

100ml low-fat natural yogurt

150g frozen raspberries

1 tablespoon honey

BEETROOT SMOOTHIE

INGREDIENTS

400ml skimmed milk

3–4 pre-cooked baby beetroots

1 ripe banana

30g porridge oats

A squirt of honey

GREEN SMOOTHIE

INGREDIENTS

400ml apple juice

1 banana

A good handful of spinach

A handful of green grapes

WHOLEWHEAT MUFFINS

MAKES 12

INGREDIENTS

260g wholewheat flour

½ teaspoon salt

3 teaspoons baking powder

2 medium eggs, beaten

225ml semi-skimmed milk

3 tablespoons brown sugar

2 tablespoons softened butter

A handful of raisins or other fruit (optional)

Wholewheat flour is great to have in the cupboard. I use it in all sorts of baking, especially where it is possible to either replace or combine with plain flour for a healthier option. I sometimes add in raisins to this mix, but you can experiment with other options too, like blueberries, chopped dried apricots or **whatever appeals to you.**

METHOD

1 Preheat the oven to 200°C. Line a muffin tray with muffin cases.

2 In a large mixing bowl combine the flour, salt and baking powder.

3 In a medium bowl mix the beaten eggs, milk, brown sugar and softened butter and stir well.

4 Add the wet ingredients to the dry ingredients in the large bowl and stir with a wooden spoon. Then add in the raisins or other fruit (if using).

5 Divide the mix evenly among the muffin cases. Bake for 25 minutes or until a skewer inserted in the middle comes out clean, remove from the oven and, when cool enough to handle, transfer to a cooling rack until fully cool.

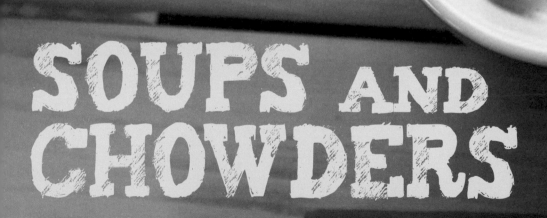

SOUPS AND
CHOWDERS

BEAUTIFUL POTATO AND LEEK SOUP

FEEDS 6

INGREDIENTS

1 large onion
4 large leeks
1 clove of garlic
2 medium potatoes
50g butter
850ml chicken stock
275ml skimmed/semi-skimmed milk
Salt and pepper to season

This is my sister Andrea's recipe and every time I go up home I look forward to having it for lunch. Served with some crusty bread this is a tasty and filling soup — **simple comfort food at its best!**

METHOD

1 Roughly chop the onion and leeks. Peel and chop the garlic. Peel and cube the potatoes.

2 In a large saucepan, over a medium heat, sweat the onion and garlic in the melted butter for 5 minutes.

3 Add the leek and sweat for a further 10 minutes, stirring occasionally to stop it sticking.

4 Add the stock, milk and potatoes and season well. Bring to the boil for 5 minutes, then simmer for another 5 minutes.

5 Allow to cool slightly, then blitz with either a hand blender or in batches in a jug blender until silky smooth. Return to the heat and once hot, serve.

BROCCOLI AND ALMOND SOUP

Another easy and very tasty soup to make. Both broccoli and almonds are packed full of great antioxidants.

INGREDIENTS

1 large onion

2 cloves of garlic

225g potatoes

1 large or 2 small heads of broccoli

75g flaked almonds

A knob of butter

A glass of dry white wine

700ml vegetable stock

150ml crème fraiche

A small bunch of parsley, coarsely chopped

FEEDS 4

METHOD

1 Chop the onion, peel and chop the garlic, peel and cut the potato into cubes and cut the broccoli into small pieces (stalk and all).

2 Gently toast the flaked almonds on a dry pan.

3 Melt the butter in a large pot and add the onion and garlic; sweat until softened but not coloured.

4 Add the potatoes and wine and bring to the boil to reduce the wine a little.

5 Add the stock and bring back to the boil, then decrease the heat and simmer for 5 minutes.

6 Add the broccoli and cook for a further 6–8 minutes, then stir in two or three teaspoons of the crème fraiche, the parsley and two or three teaspoons of the almonds.

7 Take the pot off the heat and allow to cool slightly.

8 Blend until smooth with a hand blender or in batches in a jug blender.

9 Return to the heat and stir in the rest of the crème fraiche. Once hot, serve with some toasted flaked almonds sprinkled over each bowl.

CHINESE CHICKEN AND SWEETCORN SOUP

FEEDS 6

I love this soup. Authentic Chinese food is what I aim to cook, and you can be guaranteed that the Chinese people do not eat the type of food we get in takeaways in Ireland. China does not suffer high obesity rates like Western countries do. There is a little bit more work to make this soup than some others, but it is worth it.

INGREDIENTS

1 large chicken fillet
1 litre of chicken stock
A dash of sesame oil
An inch-sized piece of ginger
200g tin of sweetcorn, drained
2 tablespoons cornflour
2 egg whites
Spring onions to garnish

METHOD

1 Poach the chicken fillet by covering it with water in a medium saucepan, placing it on a high heat until the water starts to bubble, then reducing to an easy simmer for 20 minutes until cooked and tender.

2 Remove it from the water and allow to cool on a plate, reserving the cooking water for later.

3 When the fillet is cool, shred it by pulling it into long thin strips with a fork.

4 In a large saucepan combine the stock and sesame oil, grate in the ginger and add the sweetcorn. Place on a high heat and bring to the boil.

5 In the meantime make a thin paste in a cup by mixing some of the chicken poaching water with the cornflour.

6 Beat the two egg whites lightly with another dash of the poaching water in a separate cup.

7 When the large saucepan has reached boiling point, add the shredded chicken, return to the boil and stir in the cornflour paste.

8 Now, from a height of about 15cm/6in, gently drizzle in the egg white mix while stirring (this will ensure it doesn't clump together and that it will cook fully).

9 Check for seasoning and add a pinch of salt if needed. Serve with a garnish of spring onions cut on the diagonal.

CHUNKY SEAFOOD CHOWDER

FEEDS 4

This is comfort food at its best — the smell of it alone is enough to make you want to curl up in front of a roaring fire! Choose from cod, haddock, pollock, ling, whiting, salmon, or whatever fish is available, and serve with the freshest crusty bread you can get your hands on.

INGREDIENTS

1 onion
2 sticks of celery
2 carrots
1 large potato
50g butter
50g flour
Half litre of fish or vegetable stock
Half litre of milk
200g tin of sweetcorn, drained
250g mixed fish cut into cubes
50g mussel or razor clam meat
Sea salt and black pepper to season

METHOD

1 Finely chop the onion and celery, cut the carrots into thin strips and peel and cube the potato.

2 Melt the butter in a large saucepan and add the vegetables, cook gently until softened, but not coloured.

3 Stir in the flour. Gently whisk in the stock and milk and add the sweetcorn.

4 Turn up the heat and bring to the boil, then reduce back down to a medium heat and simmer for 10 minutes.

5 Add the cubed fish and mussel/clam meat and simmer for a further 5–10 minutes.

6 Season the chowder with sea salt and fresh cracked black pepper.

7 Ladle into bowls and serve with some fresh bread.

TIP: To prepare quinoa, it should be soaked in cold water for 15 minutes before cooking, drained and rinsed again with cold water. This removes an outer coating of saponin, which has a bitter taste.

CURRIED QUINOA AND VEGETABLE SOUP

FEEDS 4

INGREDIENTS

1 onion
2 carrots
2 red peppers
1 handful of green beans
Olive oil
4 tablespoons curry paste*
200g quinoa (see tip)
800ml chicken/vegetable stock
Sea salt and black pepper to season

To me quinoa (pronounced 'Kee-no-wah') is a 'superfood'. It is readily available in most supermarkets and in all health food shops, so don't be thinking you have to trek too far to get it. It originates in South America: the Incas referred to it as 'the mother of all grains' and said that it was a sacred gift from the gods. Well, if it's good enough for the Incas it's good enough for me.

It is the most nutritious grain out there and rich in protein. It is also high in polyunsaturated fats (remember that's a good thing) and contains less carbs than most grains. It is gluten-free and contains loads of vitamins and minerals, including calcium, magnesium, zinc and iron, and is packed with antioxidants.

METHOD

1 Prepare the vegetables by dicing the onion and carrots, de-seeding and dicing the peppers and chopping the green beans into thirds.

2 Gently heat the oil in a saucepan and sauté the onion for a few minutes until softened but not coloured, then add the other vegetables and sauté for another few minutes.

3 Add in the curry paste and a splash of water, bring to the boil, then turn down to a simmer to reduce slightly, stirring frequently, for about 5 minutes. Add in the prepared quinoa (see tip) followed by the stock, then bring to the boil. Reduce the heat to a gentle simmer for about 10 minutes until the quinoa is cooked. Check the flavour and add seasoning if required.

* To make your own quick curry paste grind together 1 teaspoon of garlic powder, turmeric, cumin seeds, coriander seeds and paprika with a splash of dark soy sauce and red wine vinegar in a mortar and pestle or blitz in a small blender.

MY DAD'S
HOME-MADE SOUP

FEEDS **6**

INGREDIENTS

300g piece of beef shin
Sea salt and black pepper to season
1 onion
2 parsnips
3 carrots
3 sticks of celery
A knob of butter
150–200g dried soup mix*

Memories are something that you can hold dear forever or place somewhere quiet and go visit now and again. When I made this soup recently the memory of my dad with his glasses on his head asking, 'Has anyone seen my bloody glasses?' just came flooding back – I may as well have been standing in front of the stove years ago. This recipe is dear to me, and I hope you try it and enjoy it. You can ask your local butcher for a piece of beef shin: it is part of the foreleg that will have plenty of flavour but needs long slow cooking.

METHOD

1 Season the beef, peel and dice the onion, peel and slice the parsnips and carrots, and chop the celery.

2 In a large saucepan, sear the shin in the butter. Add in the onion and cover with a lid to soften the onion for about 5 minutes. Add the parsnips, carrots and celery and cook for a further 5 minutes to soften them.

3 Add in 1½ litres of water and bring to the boil, reduce to a steady simmer, add the dried soup mix and season. Simmer for at least 40 minutes, but the soup is at its best if allowed to simmer gently for up to two hours.

* Dried soup mix can be bought in all supermarkets. It is a mix of pearl barley, dried split peas, red lentils, etc. – great for beefing up soups to make them more filling.

NETTLE SOUP

INGREDIENTS

½ carrier bag full of nettle tops or
   young small nettles
2 medium red onions
2 carrots
2 sticks of celery
1 clove of garlic
A knob of butter
1 litre of chicken stock
Sea salt and black pepper to season
A pinch of nutmeg
3 rice cakes
2 tablespoons crème fraiche
Small bunch of chives or parsley
   chopped

FEEDS 4–6

Nettles are those 'stingy things' in the hedge that are the bane of our childhood Nettles, however, are a 'superfood', and are packed full of nutrients that strengthen the immune system and can enrich and purify the blood, which can help with good circulation, not to mention their cancer-fighting antioxidants. Not just a humble weed now, is it? Nettle soup is a lovely flavoursome soup and the main ingredient is free! Young nettles are so sweet and in spring the countryside is full of them. Use only young nettles or the tops of bigger ones.

METHOD

1 Wash the nettles thoroughly and cut out any thick stalks (wearing gloves!). Roughly peel and chop the onions, carrots, celery and garlic.

2 Gently melt the butter in a saucepan and sweat the vegetables for about 5–10 minutes to soften them.

3 Add the stock and the nettles and bring to the boil for 5 minutes until the nettles are tender, then season with salt, pepper and nutmeg.

4 Take the soup off the heat and allow it to cool slightly. Crumble in the rice cakes and purée until smooth with a stick blender, or alternatively purée in a few batches in a jug blender, adding a rice cake to each batch.

5 Pour the blended soup back into a clean saucepan and return to a medium heat, add the crème fraiche and stir until incorporated, taste and season further if required.

6 Serve with a little more crème fraiche on top, a sprinkling of the chopped herbs and some nice crusty bread. This soup can also be served cold on a nice sunny spring day.

PEAR AND PARSNIP SOUP

INGREDIENTS

1 large onion
3 cloves of garlic
2–3 sticks of celery
2 medium to large potatoes
3 large parsnips
Rapeseed oil
Sea salt and black pepper to season
700ml chicken or vegetable stock
3–4 medium pears
½ teaspoon nutmeg
1 level teaspoon cinnamon
Parsley to garnish

FEEDS 4–6

This soup may look pale, but it is brimming with flavour. There are natural sugars in both pears and parsnips, but the key word here is 'natural'.

METHOD

1 Peel and roughly chop the onion and garlic, trim and chop the celery, peel and chop the potatoes and parsnips.

2 Place a large saucepan over a medium heat and add a decent splash of rapeseed oil. To this add the onion and garlic and sweat off for a few minutes, stirring frequently, to soften but not colour. Now add the celery and cook for a further 2 minutes, then add the potatoes and parsnips with a good pinch of salt and pepper and stir for a further 2 minutes.

3 Add in the stock, turn the heat up high and bring to the boil. When the stock starts to boil, turn the heat down to a steady simmer for 10 minutes.

4 Core and chop the pears (no need to peel), then add them to the saucepan with the nutmeg and cinnamon and stir well. Allow to simmer for a further 10 minutes.

5 Remove from the heat and allow to cool slightly before blitzing with either a hand blender, or in batches in a jug blender, returning to a clean saucepan to reheat. Check the seasoning and adjust if needed.

6 Garnish with chopped parsley and serve with fresh bread of your choice.

POLLOCK AND TOMATO CHOWDER

Pollock is a more sustainable fish compared to cod or haddock, as it hasn't been as widely fished, and it is very similar to cod in flavour — so much so that it has emerged in recent years that pollock has been sold in various places as 'cod'.

INGREDIENTS

2 medium onions

2 medium carrots

2 large potatoes

2–3 sticks of celery

1 green pepper

Rapeseed oil

A sprig of thyme and a bay leaf
   tied together

400g tin of chopped tomatoes

900ml fish or vegetable stock

Black pepper

A few dashes of Tabasco sauce

600g pollock fillets

Sea salt

A bunch of parsley

FEEDS 4

METHOD

1 Peel and chop the onions, carrots and potatoes, chop the celery and de-seed and slice the green pepper.

2 Heat the oil in a large saucepan and when hot add the onion and celery. Cook until softened, then add the carrots, potatoes, pepper and tied herbs. Cook for a further 6–7 minutes, then add in the chopped tomatoes and stock.

3 Bring to the boil, then reduce to a steady simmer for 8 minutes. Add some black pepper and a few dashes of Tabasco sauce.

4 Season the pollock fillets with sea salt and black pepper and lay them on top of the vegetables in the saucepan, cover with a lid and continue to simmer for 3–4 minutes until the fish is cooked through.

5 Using a wooden spoon, gently break up the fish into chunks into the broth.

6 Divide the chowder between four bowls and serve with some freshly chopped parsley on top.

SPICY RED LENTIL AND SWEET POTATO SOUP

INGREDIENTS

1 medium onion

1 fat clove of garlic

A knob of butter

2 medium carrots

2 sticks of celery

2 large sweet potatoes (about 400g in total)

½ teaspoon cayenne pepper

½ teaspoon cumin seeds

1 litre of vegetable or chicken stock

200g split red lentils

FEEDS 4–6

Red lentils are a great source of protein and along with the sweet potato this proves a very healthy soup to have at lunchtime. There is no need to fill up on bread either as you will find the lentils are filling enough.

METHOD

1 Chop the onion and garlic and gently sweat them in a large saucepan with a knob of butter over a medium heat.

2 In the meantime peel and chop the carrots, trim and chop the celery and scrub (no need to peel) and chop the sweet potatoes into 5cm/2in cubes.

3 When the onion and garlic have softened but not coloured, add in the carrots, celery and potatoes and sweat for another few minutes.

4 Add in the cayenne pepper and cumin seeds and mix to coat the vegetables well. Then add in the stock and the lentils, bring the saucepan to the boil and reduce to a simmer for 15 minutes.

5 Once the potatoes are cooked remove the saucepan from the heat and allow to cool slightly. Then, using a hand-blender, carefully blitz the soup until smooth. If it is a little thick just add some hot water while blending. Alternatively the soup can be blended in a jug blender in batches.

6 Return to a medium/high heat to reheat fully before serving.

LUNCH

AVOCADO AND CHICKPEA SALSA WITH FRIED WHITE FISH

INGREDIENTS

2 ripe avocados

125g tinned chickpeas, rinsed

250g cherry tomatoes, quartered

1 red chilli, de-seeded and finely sliced

A small bunch of coriander leaves

1 teaspoon lime juice

Sea salt and black pepper to season

2 tablespoons plain flour

8 small fillets of white fish

Rapeseed oil

Rocket leaves and salad dressing (see p. 273) to serve

FEEDS 4

An easy salsa with a simple piece of fried fish leads to a delicious lunch. Try and source a good fresh fish supplier and stick with them. I use something like whiting or sea bream, as they are not too expensive and quite mild in flavour.

METHOD

1 Halve, de-stone and chop the avocados and add to a large mixing bowl along with the rinsed chickpeas, the cherry tomatoes, chilli, coriander leaves and lime juice. Season the mix with sea salt and fresh ground black pepper and set aside.

2 Put the flour on a plate and season it well with sea salt and fresh ground black pepper. Wash the fish fillets if necessary and pat dry with some kitchen paper, then roll them in the flour, ensuring an even, light coating.

3 Heat a non-stick frying pan with a little a glug of rapeseed oil on a medium/ high heat. When hot add the fish fillets – normally just two at a time to ensure even cooking. Cook for 2–3 minutes each side until cooked through.

4 When cooked, set aside on some kitchen paper until ready to serve. Serve the fish fillets with the salsa over the top. Some lightly dressed rocket makes a nice addition to this.

TIP: Keep the stock warm in a separate saucepan on a low/medium heat. This cuts cooking time and makes the risotto come together better.

BACON, LEEK AND PEA RISOTTO

FEEDS 4–6

INGREDIENTS

2 shallots
2 cloves of garlic
3 medium leeks
Low-fat cooking spray
100g bacon lardons
200g pearl barley
700ml warm chicken stock
A handful of frozen peas
1 tablespoon low-fat cream cheese
Black pepper to season

This is a healthy risotto as I use low-fat cooking spray instead of butter and low-fat cream cheese instead of mascarpone, which is quite heavy on the calories. But the main change is the rice ... or lack of it. Instead of using the traditional Arborio rice, I use pearl barley as it has less carbs and a lot more fibre. It takes slightly longer to absorb the stock, but only a few minutes. The sweetness of the leeks and peas really make this mouth-watering! Risottos can be intimidating; however, all they really take is some attention, but that care will lead to a wonderful meal. Bacon lardons are diced streaky and back bacon pieces; they can be bought in most supermarkets or alternatively dice up some thick bacon rashers.

METHOD

1 Peel and finely chop the shallots and garlic, wash and finely slice the leeks. Spray some low-fat cooking spray into a large saucepan and fry off the bacon lardons, crisping them up, then remove them from the saucepan and remove the excess oil with kitchen paper. Add another spray of oil and gently fry off the shallots and garlic for 2 minutes, add the leeks and sweat for 3–4 minutes.

2 Pour in the pearl barley and stir around for a minute to gently toast, then add in a ladle and a half of the warm stock. Stir until this has absorbed, then pour in another ladle of stock and add the peas.

3 Continue adding the stock ladle by ladle, letting each ladleful be absorbed before adding the next, until all the stock has all been added and absorbed.

4 Remove the risotto from the heat, add the bacon lardons and low-fat cream cheese, and stir until it has mixed through.

5 Season with cracked black pepper, stir well and serve immediately.

BAKED CHICKEN THIGHS WITH SWEET POTATOES AND CHICKPEAS

INGREDIENTS

2 red onions
600g sweet potatoes
12 cherry tomatoes
2 cloves of garlic
Rapeseed oil
8 chicken thigh fillets or 4 chicken
   legs, skinned and boned
Sea salt and black pepper to season
400g tin of chickpeas, rinsed
A bunch of parsley

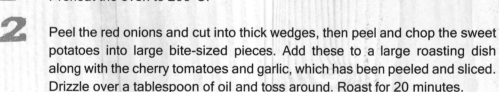

FEEDS 4

Sweet potatoes are healthier than the humble spud and, in my opinion, tastier. Even better, they take a shorter time to cook. I just love this one-dish wonder — the flavour that comes from the dark chicken meat seeps into the rest of the dish giving you a warm welcoming pat on the back: 'Well done my son.'

METHOD

1 Preheat the oven to 200°C.

2 Peel the red onions and cut into thick wedges, then peel and chop the sweet potatoes into large bite-sized pieces. Add these to a large roasting dish along with the cherry tomatoes and garlic, which has been peeled and sliced. Drizzle over a tablespoon of oil and toss around. Roast for 20 minutes.

3 In the meantime season the chicken with salt and black pepper. Heat a large frying pan on a high heat with a tablespoon of oil and when hot brown off the chicken in a few batches (so that it is brown rather than braised). Add the chicken to the oven dish and bake for another 15 minutes.

4 Remove the oven dish, add the rinsed chickpeas along with the parsley and toss around for a minute until heated through.

5 Serve with a simple side salad.

BALSAMIC CHICKEN AND CHORIZO

INGREDIENTS

Olive oil
4 medium chicken fillets
Sea salt and black pepper to season
A finger length piece of chorizo sausage
1 large onion
1 red, 1 green and 1 yellow pepper
2 garlic cloves
100ml chicken stock
5 tablespoons balsamic vinegar
1 teaspoon dried mixed herbs

This is a quick, no fuss meal. It's quite healthy served with steamed broccoli or couscous. Alternatively, if you fancy the less healthy version, you can have it with pan-fried potatoes or sweet potato wedges.

METHOD

1 Preheat the oven to 180°C. Drizzle some oil in a roasting dish, then cut the chicken fillets in half lengthways, season them with sea salt and black pepper, and place in the tray. Slice the chorizo and add to the tray.

2 Peel and slice the onion, de-seed the peppers and cut into thin strips. Bang the garlic cloves with the back of knife to release the flavour but leave them whole.

3 Put a splash of oil in a pan and add the sliced onion, then stir-fry for a few minutes until softened. Add in the peppers and garlic, fry for another minute, then tip the mixture over the chicken in the roasting dish.

4 Pour over the stock and balsamic vinegar, sprinkle over the herbs and roast in the oven for 30 minutes. Halfway through the cooking time, give it all a good stir around and spoon the juices over the top.

5 Check that the chicken is cooked through before serving.

BREADED CHICKEN SALAD

INGREDIENTS

FEEDS 2

2 chicken legs, skin on
2 slices of fresh (nice) bread, cut into cubes
Olive oil
Sea salt and black pepper to season
A handful of rocket leaves
A handful of spinach leaves
1 little gem lettuce
2 spring onions, sliced
A few mint leaves, shredded
Half a pepper, diced

1 carrot and 1 courgette cut in ribbons with
   a vegetable peeler
500ml sunflower oil
Flour for coating
2 eggs, whisked
A large handful of breadcrumbs
Ground paprika
A few shavings of Parmesan cheese

DRESSING

For a choice of dressings see pp. 273–4

METHOD

1 Preheat the oven to 200°C. Place the chicken legs in an ovenproof dish along with the bread cubes, drizzle with a little olive oil and season with salt and pepper. The bread will soak up the lovely juices that leak from the chicken during cooking. Roast for about 45 minutes in the oven until the chicken is cooked through. If some of the croutons are not crispy, place them back in the oven until they are.

2 When the chicken is cooked pull it away from the bone in large strips/chunks. Discard the skin at this point, as it has served its purpose in keeping the meat moist.

3 Wash all the leaves and dry them in a salad spinner and place in a bowl along with the spring onions, shredded mint leaves, diced pepper and ribboned carrot and courgette, and toss around.

4 To make the breaded chicken, pour about an inch depth of sunflower oil into a large saucepan and bring to a shimmering heat. Put the flour, whisked egg and breadcrumbs into three separate dishes.

5 Sprinkle the chicken pieces with ground paprika, then coat in the flour, dip in the whisked egg and then in the breadcrumbs. Make sure they are fully covered in breadcrumbs, then lower them carefully into the hot oil. You can cook a few pieces at a time. Turn over after a minute, when golden, then remove after another minute. Repeat for the remaining pieces of chicken.

6 Combine the salad, chicken and croutons on a plate or bowl and serve with shavings of Parmesan cheese and the dressing of your choice.

BUCKWHEAT SALAD

Buckwheat is a fantastic substitute for carbs such as rice or potatoes or pasta. It is rich in protein, magnesium and iron and contains rutin, a substance that protects the heart. Buckwheat is also gluten free.

INGREDIENTS

120g buckwheat
1 red pepper
Half a cucumber
A small tin of pineapple chunks in juice
Feta cheese
Black pepper to season

FEEDS 2

METHOD

1 Rinse the buckwheat in cold water in a fine sieve and place in a medium saucepan. Add 400ml of cold water and a pinch of salt. Bring the water to the boil, then reduce to a gentle simmer and cook uncovered until all the water is absorbed – this takes about 20 minutes.

2 In the meantime de-seed and dice the pepper, dice the cucumber and drain the tin of pineapple chunks.

3 When the buckwheat is cooked, fluff it through with a fork. Put it in a mixing bowl and add the diced pepper, cucumber and the pineapple chunks. Mix gently but thoroughly.

4 Divide out between two serving plates, crumble some feta cheese over the top and season with a good pinch of black pepper before serving.

COURGETTE CARBONARA

Last summer I had an abundance of courgettes and wanted to use them up. This is by no means a classic Carbonara, but it is my version and I simply love it.

INGREDIENTS

400g pasta of your choice
4 rashers of streaky bacon
Olive oil
1 small onion
1 fat clove of garlic
2 large courgettes

150g button mushrooms
1 heaped tablespoon low-fat crème fraiche
1 heaped tablespoon low-fat cream cheese
2 egg yolks, beaten
50g Parmesan cheese, grated
Black pepper to season

FEEDS 4

METHOD

1 Put the pasta on to cook according to the packet instructions.

2 Cut up the bacon and fry it in a large saucepan with a splash of oil.

3 Peel the onion and garlic and chop finely. Chop the courgette into bite-sized pieces and slice the mushrooms.

4 When the bacon is nice and crispy add the garlic and onion and fry for a further 2–3 minutes. When the onion has softened, add in the courgettes and mushrooms and fry until softened.

5 In a mixing bowl combine the crème fraiche, cream cheese, egg yolks and half the grated Parmesan cheese. Beat it all together and season well with black pepper. If it seems a bit thick add a splash of skimmed milk.

6 When the pasta is al dente, strain it in a colander in the sink, reserving a ladleful of the cooking water. Add the pasta and a splash of the reserved cooking water to the vegetables and bacon in the saucepan. Lower the heat and add the crème fraiche sauce, stirring continually for a few minutes to cook the egg yolks through without scrambling them.

7 Serve in bowls while piping hot with a sprinkle of the remaining Parmesan cheese over the top.

EASY THIN-BASE PIZZA

Like most people, I have bought many different pizzas from frozen to fresh, thin base to stuffed crust. But this, to me, is by far the nicest and has proved a hit over and over. It works out so economical that I can safely say **I'll never buy a pizza again!**

INGREDIENTS

300ml skimmed milk

7g sachet of dried yeast

500g strong white flour

Pinch of salt

Olive oil

Pasta sauce – home-made or shop-bought

Cheese of your choice

Toppings of your choice

MAKES 6

METHOD

1 Heat the milk gently until lukewarm in a saucepan or in a heatproof bowl in the microwave, add the yeast and stir until dissolved.

2 Sift the flour and salt into a mixing bowl. Make a well in middle and add the milk with the dissolved yeast.

3 Mix together using a spoon – the mixture should be quite sticky.

4 Empty out onto a lightly floured work surface and knead it for 10 minutes. Add a little oil into a large clean bowl and coat the sides of the bowl with it. Put the dough into the bowl and cover with cling film for 20–30 minutes to prove (rise).

5 Punch out the air and use it right away or wrap it in cling film and keep it in the fridge.

6 Preheat the oven to its maximum temperature (usually around 250°C). Pull off a ball of dough smaller than a tennis ball and roll it out as thinly as possible, don't worry about perfect circles.

7 Pop it onto an oiled pizza tray and lightly spoon on some pasta sauce, grate over some cheese of your choice (I just use low-fat cheddar), and add the toppings of your choice. 15–20 minutes in a HOT oven will make a lovely crispy pizza.

8 Leftover dough will keep in the fridge for a few days or can be frozen in individual portions.

GRILLED HOME-MADE BEEFBURGERS

INGREDIENTS

MAKES 8

10–12 cream crackers
1 large red onion
Olive oil
1kg good quality steak mince
1 large egg
1 teaspoon caraway seeds
1 teaspoon celery salt
1 teaspoon English mustard powder
1 teaspoon garlic powder
1 teaspoon crushed black pepper
Burger buns and toppings of your choice

I'm not normally a fan of beefburgers. Even if I did take a notion to eat in a fast food joint, a burger would be the last thing I'd go for. I normally just find them bland and as for the salad they put on top ... 'Hold the raw onions, hold the thick slice of tomato and hold the full lettuce ... thanks'. These burgers, however, I love! They are seasoned, flavoured with spice and have a great texture, plus you know exactly what is going into them. I won't tell you how to dress your burger as everyone has their own likes and dislikes.

METHOD

1 In a clean tea towel bash up the cream crackers with a rolling pin to fine crumbs. This feels good!

2 Peel and finely chop the red onion. Slowly cook it in a frying pan for a few minutes with some olive oil. This will give the burgers some sweetness.

3 Add the bashed crackers, cooled red onion and mince to a large mixing bowl. Crack an egg in and add the spices and seasoning. With clean hands, get stuck in and combine everything together, scrunching it through your fingers until it is well mixed.

4 Make about eight similar-sized burgers by rolling a portion of the mix in your hands firmly, then flattening into a burger shape. Place them on a clean plate and allow to rest in the fridge for about an hour to firm up. This stops them falling apart when cooking. The burgers can be frozen at this point to use for another day.

5 Line a grill tray with tinfoil and place the rack back on top, then preheat the grill to medium/high for a few minutes. Cooking time will all depend on the thickness of your burgers, but 4–5 minutes either side works for me. Then, like any meat, rest them for a few minutes, before serving on toasted buns with your choice of dressing.

GRILLED TURMERIC CHICKEN AND COTTAGE CHEESE ROLLS

INGREDIENTS

150g tub of cottage cheese
Tabasco sauce
1 large chicken fillet
Olive oil
1 teaspoon turmeric
1 red pepper
2 crusty bread rolls
A small bunch of coriander leaves
Black pepper to season

MAKES 2

I'm not a great lover of cottage cheese, but a dash of Tabasco sauce enlivens it into a new taste altogether.

METHOD

1 Empty the cottage cheese into a small mixing bowl and add three dashes of Tabasco sauce, give it a quick stir and set aside.

2 Brush the chicken fillet with oil, then sprinkle all over with turmeric, massage it in, place onto a grill and wash your hands. Grill the chicken for 6–8 minutes each side on a medium/high heat.

3 In the meantime de-seed and thinly slice the red pepper. Halve the bread rolls lengthways; you can toast them if you like.

4 Slice the chicken when cooked through.

5 Generously spread the cottage cheese onto the cut bread on one side, place some sliced red pepper on top and then add some chicken slices. Top with a sprinkle of coriander leaves, season with black pepper and top with the other half of the roll.

LAMB
AND MUSHROOM
CROSTINI

FEEDS 2

INGREDIENTS

1 shallot
2–3 mushrooms
100g leftover cooked lamb
Rapeseed oil
Sea salt and black pepper to season
Bread of your choice
Salad leaves
Red onion chutney

This is the only time I like my lamb well done. You need the tiny pieces of lamb to be crispy and crunchy here. It makes for a simple lunch or snack, and is a great way to use up leftover lamb.

METHOD

1 Peel and finely dice the shallot. Dice the mushrooms and dice the lamb.

2 Heat a medium-sized frying pan on a medium/high heat and pour in a glug of oil. When hot add the shallot and stir until softened. Add in the diced mushrooms and lamb, and cook on the same heat for about 10 minutes until the lamb is nice and crispy. Season it with sea salt and black pepper.

3 Slice the bread and lightly toast the slices under the grill or on a griddle pan.

4 Serve the pan mix on top of the toasted bread, with some dressed, in-season salad leaves and some red onion chutney.

LAMB'S LIVER WITH CARAMELISED RED ONIONS AND COUSCOUS

FEEDS 2

If you are not used to liver or feel a little dubious about eating it, then this is a great recipe to try. Liver is very rich in iron and B vitamins, so is great for you. Couscous is a super alternative to rice or pasta.

INGREDIENTS

2 medium red onions
A knob of butter
A splash of olive oil
2 tablespoons balsamic vinegar
1 small cup couscous
Zest of 1 lemon
200g lamb's liver
Sea salt and black pepper to season
1–2 tablespoons plain flour
A small bunch of parsley
Lemon to garnish

METHOD

1 Peel and finely slice the red onions. Heat the butter and oil in a small saucepan over a medium heat and add the red onions. Cover with a lid and cook for 8–10 minutes until softened and starting to colour.

2 Remove the lid and turn the heat up high. After a minute add the balsamic vinegar and cook, stirring all the time, until it evaporates. Remove the onions from the heat. Replace the lid and set aside.

3 Place the couscous in a large, heatproof bowl and add the grated zest of the lemon. Add 1½ cups of boiling water, cover with cling film and leave to absorb the water.

4 Slice the liver into 1cm/½in thick slices, season with salt and pepper, and sprinkle with the flour, making sure the meat is coated all over.

5 Fry the liver in batches over a medium/high heat in a non-stick pan for 40 seconds–1 minute on each side, remove and keep warm in a medium heated oven.

6 Once the liver is fried and the couscous has absorbed the water you are ready to serve. Roughly chop the parsley, add half of it to the bowl of couscous and fluff it up with a fork, mixing well.

7 Serve the couscous on separate plates topped with the red onions and liver. Garnish with the remaining parsley and a wedge of lemon.

MINI LAMB
KEBABS WITH YOGURT DIP

MAKES 2

These little bite-sized kebabs are great for a relaxed lunch or you could also make them as a starter. Prepare ahead of time so that the marinade has time to infuse its flavours into the lamb. The meat needs a minimum of an hour in the fridge.

INGREDIENTS

1 small cucumber
A pinch of salt
200ml low-fat natural yogurt
Sea salt and black pepper to season
300g lamb pieces
1 large orange
2 sprigs of thyme
1 teaspoon wholegrain mustard
Olive oil
1 jar of roasted red peppers

METHOD

1 Peel and grate the cucumber with a coarse grater into a small bowl, stir in the salt and allow to sit for an hour; the salt will draw out the water from the cucumber. After the hour squeeze out the excess water from the cucumber and discard the water.

2 In a medium bowl whip up the natural yogurt with some salt and pepper and stir in the cucumber; taste to check the seasoning and adjust if needed. Cover with cling film and put in the fridge until needed.

3 Open a large sandwich bag and place the lamb in it, add the zest and juice of the orange along with the leaves from the thyme sprigs and the wholegrain mustard. Season the contents with sea salt and freshly crushed black pepper. Push the air from the bag before sealing it tight, then massage the contents of the bag making sure they're really well mixed. Allow to marinade in the fridge for at least an hour.

4 Heat an ovenproof dish for 10 minutes at 200ºC, then pour the contents of the sandwich bag into it, drizzle lightly with oil and roast for 12–15 minutes.

5 In the meantime drain the red peppers and cut into bite-sized pieces.

6 Prepare by simply skewering a piece of tender lamb and a piece of red pepper together on a cocktail stick and serve with the yogurt dip.

MUSSELS WITH BACON AND GARLIC IN CIDER

FEEDS 2

INGREDIENTS

2 large shallots
3 cloves of garlic
Olive oil
A few sprigs of thyme
100g smoky bacon, chopped
500g mussels, scrubbed and de-bearded
250ml cider
Home-made bread, a few garlic cloves and olive oil
2 tablespoons crème fraiche

Like all seafood and fish, make sure that the mussels are as fresh as possible. Don't ever be afraid to ask your fishmonger questions, whether it is about preparing or cooking whatever it is you are buying, or about its freshness. Like a good butcher, they should be able to answer your queries. Discard any raw mussels that do not close when tapped on a hard surface and any that do not open during cooking.

METHOD

1 Finely chop the shallots and garlic. Heat about 3 tablespoons of oil in a large saucepan and add the shallots, garlic and thyme leaves, and sweat for 2–3 minutes. Then add the bacon and cook for a further 2 minutes.

2 Drop in the mussels and leave for 2 minutes, then add the cider, cover with the lid and cook for a further 3 minutes, shaking occasionally, until the mussels have all opened (any that have not opened by this stage probably will not and should be discarded).

3 In the meantime slice the bread, then rub each slice with half a clove of garlic, drizzle with olive oil and toast on a hot griddle pan.

4 Remove the mussels from the pot, leaving the juices. Add the crème fraiche to the juices and place onto a high heat, stirring for 2 minutes. Divide the mussels between two bowls and divide the sauce over each portion. Serve with the garlic bread on the side.

PAN FRIED FILLET OF SEA BREAM

INGREDIENTS

FEEDS 2

1 whole sea bream, filleted
Black pepper to season
Sea salt
1 clove of garlic, peeled
A knob of butter
1 sprig of thyme
Olive oil
1 lemon

For me sea bream is just as tasty as, if not tastier than, sea bass — and it's more sustainable, so Mother Earth will love you for choosing it! However, feel free to use any white fish for this dish. You can buy a whole fish and fillet it yourself, or get your fishmonger to do it for you. I eat mine with a simple baby leaf salad and goat's cheese.

METHOD

1 Sprinkle each fillet with ground black pepper and a little sea salt on the flesh side.

2 Put a little sea salt in a pestle and mortar and add the peeled garlic clove, then grind them together into a paste. Add in the knob of butter and mix it through.

3 Pick the thyme leaves off the sprig and toss them in a little oil so they don't cook too quickly when cooking.

4 Place a large frying pan on a high heat and add the butter-paste and the thyme leaves. When the pan is hot add the fish fillets skin side down and cook for a minute or two, until the flesh has turned white halfway up. Add a squeeze of lemon and carefully flip them over and cook for a further two minutes. Don't overcook but do ensure all the flesh in the thickest part is white.

5 Serve with a nice fresh salad or some baby new potatoes.

PEPPERED BEEF AND GREEN VEGETABLE STIR-FRY

INGREDIENTS

FEEDS 2

200g rice noodles
1 medium sirloin steak
Black pepper
1 large onion
2 cloves of garlic
1 large green pepper
2 medium courgettes
½ head of broccoli
Rapeseed oil
2 tablespoons soy sauce
1 tablespoon oyster sauce
1 tablespoon honey

Putting a simple stir-fry like this together is not only speedy but also very healthy. I use lean steak, fresh vibrant green vegetables and rice noodles, which contain no fat. They contain no gluten, salt or sugar either. Rice noodles can be found in most supermarkets, but if you are having trouble finding them, they can be found in any Asian supermarket.

METHOD

1 Cook the rice noodles according to the packet's instructions.

2 Trim all excess fat from the steak and slice into thin strips, season with a generous amount of freshly crushed black pepper and set aside. Peel and slice the onion and garlic, de-seed and slice the green pepper thinly, slice the courgettes and cut the broccoli into small florets.

3 Add some rapeseed oil to a very hot wok and allow it to heat. Carefully stir-fry the beef until it is sealed all over, then remove and set aside.

4 Add another splash of oil to the wok and add in the onion and garlic and stir-fry for about 2 minutes until slightly softened. To this add the green pepper, courgettes and broccoli and stir-fry for another 3–4 minutes until cooked but not softened too much.

5 Add in the soy sauce, oyster sauce and honey, give it all a good toss and add the beef and cooked noodles. Cook for a further 2 minutes on a high heat, tossing and stirring the wok to reheat the beef and noodles.

6 Serve immediately in two large bowls.

PORK, BEETROOT AND ORANGE SALAD

FEEDS 2

What a combination we have here! The earthiness of the beets combined with the freshness of the orange just complement the pork so well. Beets are easy to grow, even in patio tubs, and are full of antioxidants and a rich source of magnesium and potassium, which benefit a healthy heart. Pork fillet is lean and rich in protein and, of course, orange is a great source of vitamin C.

INGREDIENTS

350g pork fillet, trimmed

Sea salt and black pepper to season

1 teaspoon crushed fennel seeds

Olive oil

1 large orange

1 clove of garlic

4 baby beetroot, pre-cooked

3 tablespoons cider vinegar

Seasonal leaves

METHOD

1 Preheat the oven to 200°C.

2 Season the pork fillet all over with salt, pepper and the fennel seeds. Heat a tablespoon of oil in a medium frying pan until hot and add the pork fillet, searing it until it has a nice brown colour all the way around. Then place it in an oven dish and cook in the oven for about 20 minutes.

3 While the pork is roasting, peel and segment the orange. Break the segments in half into a bowl along with any juice you can catch.

4 Finely chop or crush the peeled garlic clove, quarter the beets and set aside.

5 When the pork is cooked through, remove from the oven and allow to rest and cool.

6 Reheat the frying pan, add another splash of oil if needed and gently fry off the garlic for a minute. Add the cider vinegar and beetroot and season to taste. Add the orange segments and juice and cook for a minute or two until heated through and the liquid is reduced slightly.

7 Carve the pork into medallions and serve over some washed seasonal leaves and drizzle the contents of the pan over the top.

QUICK-FIX HUMMUS

Hummus is a great snack or light lunch served with some breadsticks, cracker bread or pitta bread ... even vegetable sticks for an ultimate health kick.

INGREDIENTS

400g can of chickpeas
1 clove of garlic
1 lemon
1 teaspoon cumin seeds
A pinch of salt
2 tablespoons extra virgin olive oil
1 teaspoon paprika

MAKES 400g

METHOD

1 Drain and rinse the chickpeas and set a few to one side to be used as a garnish.

2 Put the remaining chickpeas in a food processor, mince in the garlic and add the juice of half the lemon along with the cumin seeds, salt, oil, paprika and 5 tablespoons of water.

3 Whizz up until you get a smooth consistency.

4 Taste and add more seasoning (salt and lemon juice) if required.

5 Serve in a bowl with a sprinkling of the whole chickpeas and a little more paprika.

SALMON FISH CAKES

INGREDIENTS

250g potatoes
100g skinless salmon fillet
Sea salt and black pepper to season
1 tablespoon plain flour (plus extra for dusting)
1 egg
A small bunch of parsley
Zest of 1 lemon

FEEDS 4

I have used salmon here as my fish of choice, but feel free to play around with different fish options.

METHOD

1 Peel the potatoes and chop them into large bite-sized pieces. Place them into a saucepan of cold salted water and place on a hot hob. Bring them to the boil.

2 In the meantime season the salmon fillet and place it into a tinfoil parcel sealing it fully all around. Once the potatoes are boiling, turn down the heat to a simmer, add the tinfoil parcel to the pot and cover with a lid. Cook for a further 8 minutes – the fish will steam cook in the parcel and the potatoes will continue to cook through.

3 Remove the parcel and carefully drain the potatoes and allow them to steam dry and cool in a colander.

4 Once the potatoes have cooled, mash them in the saucepan and then transfer them to a large mixing bowl. Break in the fish and sprinkle in the tablespoon of flour. Add the egg, chopped parsley and the lemon zest. Mix this thoroughly with a wooden spoon until fully combined.

5 Flour your hands, divide the mix into four balls and then form them into fish-cakes. Place on a lightly flour-dusted plate and place in the fridge to firm up for an hour; this will stop them breaking up later when grilling.

6 Grill the fishcakes under a medium/high grill for 3–4 minutes each side to colour them and heat through. Serve with a wedge of lemon and a simply dressed salad.

SPICY BEEF WRAP

FEEDS 2

INGREDIENTS

1 medium sirloin steak, fat trimmed
Olive oil
½ teaspoon paprika
½ teaspoon dried oregano
½ teaspoon cumin seeds
1 small red pepper
2 spring onions
4 tablespoons sour cream
1 tablespoon horseradish sauce
2 low-fat tortilla wraps
Sweet chilli sauce
Fresh rocket

This is a great simple lunch that will blow your socks off. It packs a super flavour punch. Alternatively it can be made with chicken or pork, even chicken dippers for a really easy option – just substitute some low-fat mayonnaise for the horseradish and sour cream sauce.

METHOD

1 Take the steak out of the fridge 15 minutes before cooking, massage in a drop of oil and season both sides with the paprika, oregano and cumin seeds.

2 De-seed and finely slice the red pepper and the spring onions, then set aside.

3 In a small bowl combine the sour cream and horseradish sauce to use as a dip.

4 Place the steak on a screaming hot griddle pan – 2–3 minutes either side should suffice for a medium-rare steak – then remove and wrap in tinfoil to rest for a few minutes (ideally 10–15 minutes, but as long as you wish).

5 Heat up the tortilla wraps as instructed on the packaging. Spread some sweet chilli sauce on the wrap, carve the steak into thin slices and arrange half on each wrap, top with the pepper, spring onions and fresh rocket, and fold up the wrap.

6 Serve with some low-fat crisps and the horseradish dip, and, most of all, enjoy!

SPINACH AND GOAT'S CHEESE SOUFFLÉ

FEEDS 4

A soufflé is nothing to fear ... follow the recipe to the letter and you should be just fine. And if it doesn't work the first time, then try again until you get it right; everything won't work out perfect every time in cooking — hell, even in life — but it's all about trial and error, we just have to learn from our mistakes.

This is a savoury soufflé and works very well for a light lunch served with a simple side salad or as a starter course for a dinner to impress. Spinach is rich in antioxidants and packed full of vitamins and nutrients.

INGREDIENTS

Softened butter

250g baby spinach, washed

Sea salt and black pepper to season

Olive oil

1 shallot

1 clove of garlic

20g plain flour

A pinch of cayenne pepper

125ml skimmed milk

100g soft goat's cheese

1 tablespoon Parmesan cheese, grated

2 large eggs, separated

METHOD

1 Preheat the oven to 200°C. Brush four ramekins with the softened butter in upward strokes, set in a baking tray and chill for 5 minutes.

2 Place a large pan over a medium/high heat, add the spinach and season with salt and pepper. Stir for a few minutes until the leaves have wilted. Add in a small splash of water to stop it sticking if needed. Then tip the wilted spinach into a colander in the sink and allow it to cool. When cool, wrap the spinach in a clean tea towel and squeeze out any excess moisture. Chop finely and set aside.

3 In a medium saucepan, heat some oil over a medium heat. Peel and finely chop the shallot and garlic, then cook until soft. Add the flour and cayenne pepper and stir over a low heat for 3–4 minutes, then whisk in the milk slowly, bit by bit. Simmer for a few minutes until it becomes thick, then transfer to a large mixing bowl and cool slightly.

4 Crumble the goat's cheese into this mixture, add the Parmesan cheese and some salt and pepper, then stir to combine. Mix in the chopped spinach and the egg yolks and set aside.

5 In a clean mixing bowl beat the egg whites with an electric whisk to form stiff peaks. Fold this into the spinach mix until just combined.

6 Spoon the mixture into the prepared ramekins and give them a few gentle taps on the countertop to get rid of any large air pockets that may have formed. Run the tip of a small sharp knife around the edges (this will allow the soufflés to rise without sticking to the top rim) and bake for 13–15 minutes until risen and golden brown on top.

7 Serve immediately.

STEAK PITTA SAMBO

FEEDS 2

Wholewheat pitta pockets are a great alternative to doughy bread for those looking for a lighter choice.

INGREDIENTS

1 shallot
1 small clove of garlic
1 red pepper
1 sirloin steak
Olive oil
Sea salt and black pepper to season
2 large wholewheat pitta pockets
1 lemon
1 tablespoon horseradish sauce
A handful of rocket leaves

METHOD

1 Peel and finely chop the shallot and garlic, de-seed and slice the red pepper, and set aside. Trim any fat from the meat, then massage some oil onto one side and season generously with sea salt and black pepper; turn over and repeat on the other side.

2 Place a frying pan on a hot hob and let it get screaming hot. Carefully place the steak on, cook for 2–3 minutes before turning over, cook for another 2–3 minutes (for medium-rare), then remove and cover with foil to rest for about 10 minutes.

3 Turn the heat down slightly, add some oil to the pan and cook the shallot and garlic for 3–4 minutes until softened, then add the red pepper, cook for a further 3 minutes and remove from the heat.

4 Place the pitta pockets into the toaster or under a medium/high grill until warmed through.

5 In the meantime in a small mixing bowl combine a tablespoon of oil, a squeeze of lemon juice and the horseradish sauce and season with salt and pepper. Give it a whisk to combine and use this to dress the rocket leaves.

6 Carefully cut open the pitta pockets (be careful not to burn yourself on the steam coming out). Slice the steak thinly, then divide all ingredients evenly between the pitta pockets.

STUFFED TOMATOES

INGREDIENTS

4 large vine tomatoes
A handful of frozen sweetcorn
Half a red pepper, diced
1 clove of garlic, peeled and chopped
1 teaspoon dried oregano
10–12 fresh basil leaves, roughly chopped
1 cup cooked brown rice
3 tablespoons soft ricotta cheese
Sea salt and black pepper to season
Olive oil

FEEDS 2

A very low fat, low sugar recipe, but it is tasty and you can play around with the fillings yourself, choosing your own favourite flavours.

METHOD

1 Preheat the oven to 200°C.

2 Carefully cut the top off the tomatoes, about 1cm/½in down and set aside the tops. Using a small knife and teaspoon carefully cut around and scoop out the insides and discard them. Set the hollowed out tomatoes upside down on kitchen paper to drain the excess liquid.

3 Now combine the rest of the vegetables, the herbs, rice and cheese in a mixing bowl, and season with sea salt and black pepper. Spoon the mixture into the tomatoes.

4 Place the tomatoes on a non-stick baking tray and top with their lids, then drizzle everything with a little oil.

5 Cook for 20 minutes, remove the tops from the oven and set aside. Turn down the heat to 180°C and continue cooking the tomatoes for another 20–25 minutes. Replace the tops and serve up with a simple salad.

SUGAR CRUSTED LAMB CUTLETS WITH A RED WINE JUS

INGREDIENTS

4 lamb cutlets
2 tablespoons soft brown sugar
1 tablespoon English mustard powder

For the Jus

1 full glass of red wine
1 sprig of rosemary
1 garlic clove, peeled
A splash of soy sauce
A splash of balsamic vinegar
1 tablespoon honey

FEEDS 2

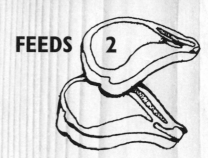

I just love lamb cutlets and the caramelised fatty bits from grilling these bad boys are just to die for! Meat on the bone is always tastier and, with the richness from the jus, these cutlets leave you wanting more and more.

METHOD

1 Pat the cutlets dry with kitchen paper (this helps the other ingredients to stick) and set aside.

2 Sprinkle the soft brown sugar and mustard powder on a plate or board and roll the chops in the mixture, pushing down and getting a good even coating all the way around.

3 Place the coated cutlets under a preheated grill on a high heat and grill them for 5–7 minutes on either side.

4 In the meantime pour the glass of wine into a small pan and add the rosemary and garlic; place it on a high heat and reduce the wine by half. Add the soy sauce, balsamic vinegar and honey, and stir through. Reduce another bit until it coats the back of a spoon. Remove the rosemary and garlic before pouring over the cutlets.

5 Serve with some steamed baby potatoes and a simple side salad.

THAI-STYLE TURKEY BURGERS

MAKES 4

INGREDIENTS

4 spring onions
1 red chilli
A thumb-sized piece of ginger, peeled
400g turkey mince
A small bunch of coriander leaves
50ml rapeseed oil
Crusty bread baps
Fresh salad leaves
Sweet chilli sauce to serve

Turkey is the leanest of meats,

so using turkey mince can wipe away some of the guilt for having a very tasty succulent burger for lunch!

METHOD

1 Thinly slice the spring onions, de-seed and slice the chilli, and grate the ginger. In a large mixing bowl combine the turkey mince, spring onions, ginger, chilli, coriander and oil. Now get in there with clean hands and start scrunching everything together until really well combined.

2 Divide the mixture into four and form into burgers. Place them on an oiled baking tray or plate, cover with cling film and refrigerate for an hour to firm up. This will ensure they keep their shape and don't fall apart when grilling.

3 Grill the burgers on just higher than medium heat for about 6–8 minutes on both sides, ensuring they are cooked through. Serve in some fresh crusty baps (toasted if you prefer) with in-season salad leaves and a generous dollop of sweet chilli sauce.

VIETNAMESE CHICKEN SALAD

INGREDIENTS

3 shallots

Half a red chilli, de-seeded

1 tablespoon granulated sugar

3–4 black peppercorns

100ml rice vinegar

3 tablespoons oyster sauce

1 large chicken fillet

Olive oil

Sea salt and black pepper to season

¼ head of white cabbage

1 large carrot

A few sprigs of mint

A small bunch of coriander

A small handful of salted peanuts

FEEDS 2

I love looking up recipes from around the world — there is a desire in me to travel and taste all the glorious recipes from the different continents. This salad came about using some basic ingredients and a little Vietnamese inspiration.

METHOD

1 Peel and coarsely chop the shallots. Put them into a large mortar and pestle along with the chopped chilli, the sugar and the black peppercorns. Grind everything together until soft and the liquid is dispersed from the shallots. Transfer this mix to a large bowl and stir in the rice vinegar and oyster sauce. Set to one side.

2 Brush the chicken fillet with oil and season with salt and pepper. Grill it under a medium/high heat for about 6–8 minutes on both sides, making sure it is cooked through. Allow to cool, then shred with your fingers finding the natural grain.

3 Finely shred the cabbage and carefully chop the carrot into fine matchsticks. Add these to the vinegar mix, toss thoroughly, then add the chicken, mint leaves and coriander leaves, toss until combined and top with a scatter of roughly chopped peanuts.

STARTERS

BEETROOT, BLACK PUDDING AND POMEGRANATE SALAD

INGREDIENTS

4–6 pre-cooked baby beetroots
1 small black pudding
Olive oil
1 pomegranate
1 lemon
A large handful of rocket
1–2 little gem lettuces
50g feta cheese
Sea salt and black pepper to season

FEEDS 2

This is epic – the earthy flavours from the beetroot and the black pudding up against the sharpness from the pomegranate, well it works ... oh it works so well!

METHOD

1 Cut the pre-cooked beetroots into quarters and slice the black pudding into 1cm/½in slices.

2 Place a medium frying pan on a medium/high heat and add a splash of oil. Fry the black pudding slices for 2 minutes, turn them over and add in the beetroot, a squeeze of pomegranate juice and a squeeze of lemon juice, then cook for a further 3 minutes until the pudding slices are cooked and the beets warmed through. Set aside.

3 In a bowl dress the rocket with a sprinkle of good olive oil. Carefully pull the leaves from the little gem lettuces, keeping them whole.

4 To serve the salad, place four little gem lettuce leaves on each plate so they look like little bowls, divide the rocket between all the 'bowls' and divide out the pudding and beets on top of the rocket. Tap out the pomegranate seeds over the dish and crumble over little wedges of the feta cheese. Season the salad with another squeeze of lemon juice and a pinch of salt and pepper.

CARAMELISED RED ONION AND CHERRY TOMATO TARTLETS

INGREDIENTS

500g pack of puff pastry
2 medium red onions
A knob of butter and a splash of olive oil
2 tablespoons balsamic vinegar
150g cherry tomatoes
1 small clove of garlic, peeled
8–10 basil leaves
1 teaspoon white wine vinegar
1 tablespoon olive oil
Sea salt and black pepper to season

MAKES 8

These little gems will bring a smile to any guest's face; they are elegant and pretty but pack a serious flavour punch.

METHOD

1 Roll out the pastry ¼cm/⅛in thick. Cut into squares roughly 8cm/3in square using a knife or pizza cutter. Don't be too fussy. Using the tip of a sharp knife score a border ¼cm/⅛in from the edge of each one, without cutting the whole way through. Place the squares on greaseproof paper on a baking sheet and pop in the fridge until needed.

2 Peel and finely slice the onions. Place a small saucepan on a medium/high heat on the hob and add the butter and oil, add in the onions, cover with a lid and cook for 8–10 minutes stirring occasionally.

3 Turn the heat up full and once the pan is hot add the balsamic vinegar. Stir until the vinegar has evaporated and the onions are nicely caramelised.

4 Preheat the oven to 200ºC.

5 Halve the cherry tomatoes, add to a mixing bowl and mince in the garlic. Roughly chop the basil leaves and add to the bowl, then add in the white wine vinegar and tablespoon of oil. Season with sea salt and black pepper and allow to marinate for 5 minutes.

6 Remove the pastry squares from the fridge and spoon some of the red onion on each, ensuring you stay within the scored border. Place the cherry tomatoes on top and drizzle over any marinade left in the bowl. Place in the preheated oven and bake for 15–20 minutes or until the pastry is golden.

GOAT'S CHEESE AND SPICED PEAR SALAD

FEEDS 4

INGREDIENTS

2 x 410g tins of quartered pears

Sprinkle of allspice or spices of your choice

A small handful of pine nuts

300g hard goat's cheese

4 handfuls of fresh rocket

Sticky Red Wine Reduction
Dressing (see p. 273)

A small handful of sun-dried tomatoes
rehydrated in boiling water (according to
packet instructions)

I tasted this in a restaurant one night and thought 'I have to make this'. It was first time I'd tasted goat's cheese … yum!! The dressing is as close as I could get after a few attempts to imitate it. I have put in the recipe to use spices of your choice — I use whatever jumps out at me when I open the cupboard. You can simply use allspice!

METHOD

1 Preheat the oven to 180°C.

2 Open and drain the pears, cut the quarters in half again and sprinkle well with spices. Place on an oiled baking tray and bung into the oven. They will take 30 minutes or so to soften up and colour slightly.

3 Toast the pine nuts.

4 Cut the goat's cheese into thick slices, place on a sheet of foil on a baking tray and grill on a medium/high heat until bubbling and coloured slightly.

5 To plate up, place a handful of rocket leaves dressed with Red Wine Reduction Dressing on the centre of the plate with slices of the goat's cheese on top. Place the spiced pears around the edges along with the rehydrated sun-dried tomatoes. Sprinkle over the toasted pine nuts and spoon over some more dressing.

HOT BUFFALO WINGS WITH BLUE CHEESE DIP

There are a few restaurants famed for their buffalo wings, but of course they have 'secret recipes'. Well, I worked on it and after a lot of trial and error I came up with this recipe — and I love it. It can't be classed as low fat, but can be a treat once in a while ... and what a treat it is!

INGREDIENTS

1 tray of chicken wings (normally contains 16)
A light sprinkle of cayenne pepper (optional)
Oil for deep frying
50g butter
6 tablespoons cider vinegar
3 tablespoons Tabasco sauce (4 if you like it hotter)
3 tablespoons tomato purée
Juice of half a lemon
A few sticks of celery to serve

FEEDS 4 AS A STARTER OR 2 AS A MAIN

For the blue cheese dip
3 tablespoons mayonnaise
3 tablespoons sour cream
1 teaspoon white wine vinegar
1 teaspoon freshly squeezed lemon juice
Finely chopped parsley
Small clove of garlic, peeled and minced
3 tablespoons crumbled blue cheese
Sea salt and black pepper to season

METHOD

1 Combine all the ingredients for the dip and place in the fridge for at least an hour.

2 The chicken wings need to be cut at the two joints (into three pieces but discard the wing tip) with a heavy, sharp knife. Sprinkle lightly with cayenne pepper if you like them extra spicy.

3 Deep fry in batches for about 10 minutes per batch until cooked through and nice and crispy; they can be kept in a warm oven until all the batches are deep fried (I usually do them in three batches).

4 In the meantime in a saucepan gently melt the butter, then add the cider vinegar, Tabasco sauce and tomato purée and whisk it together until combined. Squeeze in the juice of half a lemon at the end.

5 Place the cooked wings in a large bowl and pour over the sauce and toss to give a good even coat.

6 Serve with the cooling blue cheese dip and a few sticks of celery.

ROASTED RED PEPPER AND BLACK OLIVE SALAD

INGREDIENTS

2 large red peppers
Olive oil
A large sprig of thyme (or marjoram or oregano)
1 small shallot
A small handful of pitted black olives
Black pepper
Good balsamic vinegar

FEEDS 2 AS A STARTER OR LUNCH OR 4 AS A SIDE

'A salad without salad leaves? It's preposterous!' Sometimes we have to think outside the box. As well as a tasty starter, this is a great light lunch with some crusty bread, or it can be served as a side dish with a good steak or grilled fish.

METHOD

1 Preheat the oven to 200°C.

2 Halve the peppers lengthways and de-seed them. Place them on an oiled baking tray, cut side down, and pop them in the oven for 20–25 minutes until charred. Remove them and, while still hot, transfer them to a large bowl and immediately cover with cling film and allow to cool for about 10–15 minutes.

3 In the meantime pick the leaves off the thyme, finely dice the shallot and halve the pitted olives.

4 When the peppers are cool, peel off the skins; don't worry if a little remains. Slice the peppers into long thin slices and place in a serving bowl. Season with some freshly cracked black pepper.

5 Add in the thyme leaves, shallot and olives and generously drizzle over the balsamic vinegar.

6 Allow to cool fully before serving.

STICKY BACON RIBS

INGREDIENTS

1kg bacon ribs

For the marinade

4 tablespoons olive oil

2 tablespoons red wine vinegar

2 tablespoons dark soy sauce

1 tablespoon fish/oyster sauce

1 tablespoon Worcestershire sauce

5 tablespoons honey

1 teaspoon Chinese five-spice

1 teaspoon chopped sage

1 tablespoon cayenne pepper

A few cloves of garlic, peeled

A big pinch of black pepper

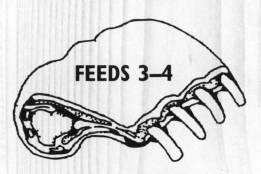

FEEDS 3–4

These ribs are a wonderful snack or a starter for a meal. They can also be started off in the oven and finished off on a BBQ for that lovely smoky flavour.

METHOD

1 If the ribs are still in a rack, carefully cut down between the bones to separate.

2 Mix all the ingredients for the marinade in a mixing bowl. Place the ribs in an even layer on a large roasting tray and pour over the marinade. Toss the ribs so they are all well coated. Cover with cling film and place in the fridge for as long as possible. Marinade for at least an hour but preferably overnight to let all the wonderful flavours combine and infuse into the meat.

3 When you're ready for cooking, preheat the oven to 200ºC. Cook the ribs for 35 minutes, take them out halfway through cooking and give them a toss around. You can then finish off on a BBQ or under the grill to caramelise the sticky marinade.

4 Serve with some lightly stir-fried vegetables of your choice.

STUFFED POTATO SKINS

These wee beauties make a great starter or you can add a side salad for a great lunch. This is the combination I use, but you should use your imagination and experiment. This is a great way of using up the leftover meat you strip off a cooked chicken. We are sometimes a little bit too quick to throw out the roast chicken carcass without taking a few minutes to fully strip it down ... there is always another small meal left with the use of a little imagination.

FEEDS 4 AS A STARTER OR 2 AS LUNCH

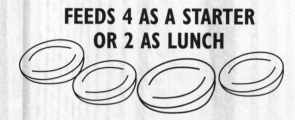

INGREDIENTS

4 medium/large rooster potatoes
A large handful of leftover chicken, shredded
1 red pepper
2 tablespoons sour cream
2 teaspoons pesto (see p. 282)
12–14 basil leaves
Sea salt and black pepper to season
Olive oil for brushing
Parmesan cheese

METHOD

1 Scrub and carefully stab the potatoes all over with a small sharp knife. You can bake them for 45–50 minutes in a hot oven (200°C) or for 10–12 minutes in a microwave until soft.

2 Meanwhile, place the shredded chicken in a large mixing bowl. De-seed and finely slice the red pepper and add it to the bowl.

3 Add the sour cream and pesto. Roughly chop the fresh basil leaves and add to the bowl. Season well with plenty of black pepper and a pinch of salt and stir with a wooden spoon until well combined. Set aside.

4 When the potatoes are cooked through and cool enough to handle, slice them evenly in half. Scoop out the flesh using a teaspoon, leaving a thin layer of potato (keep the flesh to use in another recipe).

5 Using some flavoured or plain oil, brush a light coat all over both sides of the potato halves, set them skin side up on a grill and carefully grill them on a medium/high heat for a few minutes until crispy – be careful not to burn them. Turn them over and do the same, lightly crisping the insides.

6 Spoon the chicken mixture into the potato skins, grate a little Parmesan cheese over the top and place back under the grill until the filling is heated through and the cheese is bubbling on top.

7 Serve right away.

DINNERS

BEEF AND GUINNESS PIE

How 'diddly-dee' Irish, I know ... but if it's good, it's good. There is a deep richness of flavour that comes from the Guinness that enriches everything else without overpowering it.

INGREDIENTS

500g stewing steak pieces
2 heaped tablespoons plain flour
Sea salt and black pepper to season
1 large onion
2 carrots
2 parsnips

3 sticks of celery
Rapeseed oil
500ml can of Guinness
500g pack of puff pastry
1 egg, beaten

FEEDS 4

METHOD

1 Pat the steak pieces dry with kitchen paper. Put the flour on a plate and season it with a generous pinch of sea salt and black pepper, then roll the steak pieces in the seasoned flour until fully covered in a good coating. Shake off any excess flour.

2 Peel and chop the onion, carrots and parsnips and wash and chop the celery, then set aside.

3 In a large saucepan heat 2 tablespoons of oil over a high heat, add the steak pieces in small batches to brown them all over before removing, with a slotted spoon, onto kitchen paper.

4 When all the meat is browned, carefully wipe down the saucepan with kitchen paper and return to a medium heat. Add a tablespoon of oil and fry the onion until softened but not coloured, then add in the carrots, parsnips and celery. Fry these for 8–10 minutes, then add the beef back in along with all of the Guinness.

5 Bring the saucepan to the boil, then cover and reduce to a steady simmer for 45 minutes.

6 Preheat the oven to 180°C. Pour the contents of the saucepan carefully into an ovenproof dish.

7 Roll out the puff pastry and cover the dish with it, pressing around the edges and trimming off the excess. Pierce a few times with a sharp knife and brush over with the beaten egg to give it colour.

8 Place in the oven and bake for 35–40 minutes until the pastry is golden and delicious.

9 Serve with some mashed potatoes for a warm hearty meal.

BEEF BOURGUIGNON

INGREDIENTS

3–4 rashers of streaky bacon
Olive oil
900g lean braising steak
2 onions, chopped
1 tablespoon plain flour
300ml good red wine
300ml beef stock
115g button mushrooms
A bouquet garni of herbs (bay, rosemary and thyme)
Sea salt and black pepper to season
Parsley to garnish

FEEDS 4

Beef Bourguignon (or Boeuf Bourguignon) is a French classic; it is very rich in flavour and is ideally served with creamy mashed potatoes.

METHOD

1 Preheat the oven to 160°C.

2 Chop the bacon and fry in a non-stick frying pan in a little oil until lightly browned. When cooked, remove with a slotted spoon and pat off the excess oil with kitchen paper, then add to a casserole pot.

3 Using the same pan and a little more oil if needed, fry the beef in small batches to brown it and transfer to the casserole pot.

4 Reduce the heat slightly and, again in the same pan, fry the onions until softened. Transfer these to the casserole pot using a slotted spoon.

5 Stir the flour into the remaining oil in the pan. Gradually whisk in the wine and stock and bring to the boil, stirring to make sure it is smooth. Add the mushrooms and bouquet garni, season with salt and pepper and pour into the casserole pot.

6 Cover with the lid and place in the oven for 2 hours until the meat is very tender and the sauce thickened slightly.

7 Serve with creamy mash and a garnish of fresh parsley.

TIP: Get your fishmonger to skin and bone the fish fillets.

BEER BATTERED
FISH 'N' CHIPS

FEEDS 4

INGREDIENTS

4 medium fillets of white fish
  (cod, haddock, whiting, etc.)
Sea salt and black pepper to season
1kg scrubbed potatoes, skins left on
225g plain flour, plus some for coating
3 heaped tablespoons bicarbonate of soda
284ml good beer/lager
1 litre of vegetable oil
1 lemon

Home-made fish 'n' chips can sound and feel daunting until you actually try it out. I can promise that after you see how easy and tasty it is you'll be hooked — excuse the pun. The fish and chips are deep fried, so this wouldn't be a dinner for every night of the week but rather a treat now and again. Served with minted mushy peas (see p. 215) — it is a classic combination that won't disappoint.

METHOD

1 Cut the fillets into 5cm/2in-wide strips, making sure they are free of bones. Season with a pinch of salt and a generous amount of black pepper and set aside.

2 Preheat the oven to 150°C.

3 Cut the potatoes into thin chips, skins and all.

4 To make the batter, sift the flour into a mixing bowl, add a pinch of salt and the bicarbonate of soda. Pour in the beer/lager and whisk together – you are looking for a double cream consistency. Allow it to foam up or rise.

5 Half fill a wok with vegetable oil and put it on a medium/high heat (it shouldn't get too hot too quickly).

6 Pop a chip in to test the oil – if it rises to the top the oil is ready. Remove the chip. Dip a piece of fish into a shallow bowl of flour, coating it all over, then straight into the batter, again coating it fully. Carefully lower it into the hot oil. You can cook two or three pieces at the one time. Give them a few minutes and turn them over in the oil using kitchen tongs. Once golden on both sides, remove carefully onto a baking tray and pop into the oven – this will finish off the cooking and dry off some of the oil making the batter dry and crispy. Repeat for the remainder of the fish.

7 Once the fish pieces are all in the oven, put the chips carefully into the same oil. When they're golden remove using a large slotted spoon. Serve with a wedge of lemon and, of course, salt and vinegar.

TIP: Keep the stock warm in a separate saucepan on a low/medium heat. It cuts cooking time and makes the risotto come together better.

BUTTERNUT SQUASH, SAGE AND CRISPY BACON RISOTTO

INGREDIENTS

1 butternut squash
2 shallots
2 cloves of garlic
8–10 sage leaves
Olive oil
200g Arborio rice
1 glass dry white wine
700ml chicken or vegetable stock
8 rashers of streaky bacon
1 tablespoon low-fat cream cheese
Black pepper to season

FEEDS 2

This is comfort food at its best. I use the term comfort food a lot and I mean the type of food that just makes you feel all warm and satisfied, that kicks a winter's evening up the arse, that, as my father used to say, 'would warm the cockles of your heart'. I just think that butternut squash is an unsung hero as it is a wonderfully versatile vegetable and keeps so well in storage without going off. It helps protect against cancer, heart disease and mental dysfunction, and also encourages healthy skin, muscles and nerves ... in other words give it a cape and red underpants and you have an all-round hero!

METHOD

1 Peel and halve the butternut squash lengthways. Using a spoon scoop out the seeds and fibres from the cavity of each half and discard. Carefully cut the butternut squash into small bite-sized cubes – I say carefully because it can be quite tough to cut through when uncooked!

2 Peel and dice the shallots and garlic as finely as possible and roll up and chop the sage leaves.

3 Heat a tablespoon of oil in a large saucepan over a medium heat and gently fry the shallots and garlic for 2 minutes. Add in the chopped sage and fry off for a further 2 minutes.

4 Pour in the rice and stir around for a minute to gently toast, turn up the heat a little and add the wine. Stir frequently and once the wine is absorbed add the cubed squash, then add a ladle and a half of the stock. Again, stir frequently until the stock is absorbed. Pour in another ladle of the stock and repeat. Continue adding the stock ladle by ladle, each time it is fully absorbed.

5 In the meantime crisp up the bacon under a hot grill for 2–3 minutes on each side, then set aside on some kitchen paper.

6 When the stock is all absorbed in the risotto, remove it from the heat and stir in the low-fat cream cheese, season with freshly crushed black pepper and divide between two bowls. Cut up the bacon with clean scissors and sprinkle it over the top.

CAULIFLOWER AND CHEESE PASTA BAKE

FEEDS 4–6

INGREDIENTS

½ head of cauliflower
100g low-fat cheddar cheese
100g Parmesan cheese
A bunch of parsley
400g pasta of your choice
200g crème fraiche
Sea salt and black pepper to season

This is my take on what the Yanks would call 'Mac 'n' Cheese'. It is a filling, tasty and relatively economical meal ... great for filling up kids while sneaking some healthy, antioxidant-rich cauliflower in there too.

METHOD

1. Cut the cauliflower head into small florets and finely chop the stalk (don't waste it!). Grate the two cheeses and chop the parsley finely.

2. Bring a large pot of salted water to the boil and add the pasta and cauliflower.

3. Cook according to the pasta packet's instructions.

4. In the meantime place a heatproof bowl over a pot of simmering water, making sure the water doesn't touch the bottom of the bowl. Add in the crème fraiche and give it a good stir. Then gently melt the cheddar and the Parmesan cheese into the crème fraiche and after that add the chopped parsley and season with the salt and pepper. Remove the bowl from the heat with a pair of oven gloves – beware of the steam – and set aside.

5. When the pasta and cauliflower are cooked, drain in a colander, reserving the cooking water.

6. Return the pasta and cauliflower to the pot and place onto the heat, add in the crème fraiche mixture and stir in well. Add in a splash or two of the cooking water to loosen it all up a bit.

7. You can serve it like this, wet and gooey, or transfer to an oven dish and place under a hot grill for a few minutes to crisp up the top, making it golden and gorgeous!

CHICKEN KASHMIRI

This is moist and tender chicken at its best, in an aromatic, spicy yogurt sauce. It can be a one-pot wonder or, to bulk it up for a crowd, serve it with brown rice. Feel free to add in some more veg like peppers, carrots or broccoli. This is yet another healthy meal brimming with flavour.

FEEDS 4

INGREDIENTS

4 medium chicken fillets
200g baby potatoes
1 onion, peeled
4 cloves of garlic, peeled
1 chilli, de-seeded
2-inch piece of ginger, peeled
Olive oil
1 teaspoon cumin seeds

1 teaspoon coriander seeds
Seeds from 2 cardamom pods
300ml chicken stock
2 handfuls of baby spinach
Sea salt and black pepper to season
300g low-fat natural yogurt
Bunch of fresh coriander
1 lemon

METHOD

1 Cut the chicken fillets into cubes. Quarter the potatoes, unpeeled. Finely chop the onion, garlic, chilli and ginger.

2 Heat a splash of oil in a large, lidded pan. Stir-fry the chicken for a few minutes, ensuring it is golden on the edges and white all over.

3 In the meantime bash the cumin, coriander and cardamom seeds in a mortar and pestle.

4 When the chicken is ready add in the potatoes, onion, spices, garlic, chilli and ginger and fry for a further 3–4 minutes. Add in the stock and bring to the boil, put the lid on and simmer gently for 20 minutes until the potatoes are cooked, the chicken is super tender and the sauce has thickened.

5 Stir in the spinach and season. Take off the heat and allow it to cool slightly. Pour in the yogurt and stir until blended in.

6 Serve with a scattering of coriander leaves and a wedge of lemon.

CURRIED CHICKPEAS AND CAULIFLOWER

INGREDIENTS

1 medium onion
A thumb-sized piece of ginger
2 cloves of garlic
Olive oil
1 tablespoon granulated sugar
¼ teaspoon turmeric
¼ teaspoon cayenne pepper
2 tablespoons balsamic vinegar
1 medium head of cauliflower
300g tinned chickpeas
A handful of raisins
2 handfuls of baby spinach

FEEDS 4

This is a very simple vegetarian option.
Serve with some basmati rice and maybe some naan breads.

METHOD

1 Peel and finely slice the onion, peel and dice both the ginger and garlic.

2 Heat a splash of oil in a large saucepan and gently fry the onion with the sugar over a medium/high heat for about 6–8 minutes until the onion starts to colour. Add the ginger, garlic, turmeric, cayenne pepper and the balsamic vinegar, and cook for a further 8 minutes on a medium heat, stirring occasionally.

3 In the meantime, cut the cauliflower into florets and drain the chickpeas and give them a good rinse in a sieve under the cold tap. Add these to the saucepan along with the raisins and 150ml of water. Cook for 20 minutes covered with a lid.

4 Add in the spinach and cook for a few minutes more until it has wilted.

5 Serve with some freshly cooked basmati rice.

CURRY CHINESE STYLE

I have noticed that most of the curry recipes in cook books are Indian-style curries, but I prefer Chinese curry so I taught myself to cook this one. This is a vegetable curry because, let's face it, we don't need meat in all our dishes and this is a great way of eating veg because the curry flavours stand out more than the veg. Choose whatever veg you like — I normally go for cauliflower, butternut squash, mushrooms and courgettes, and trust me, you won't even miss the meat! This recipe is for the sauce alone, the rest is up to you!

INGREDIENTS

6 tablespoons vegetable oil
3 onions, finely chopped
A thumb-sized piece of ginger, peeled
   and thinly sliced
4 cloves of garlic, sliced
4 mild fleshy red chillies, seeds
   removed and chopped

½ teaspoon turmeric
½ teaspoon ground cumin
½ teaspoon ground coriander
½ tablespoon chilli powder
2½ teaspoons curry powder
2½ tablespoons plain flour
400–500ml vegetable stock
Vegetables of your choice cut into
   bite-sized pieces
1 teaspoon onion seeds

FEEDS 4

METHOD

1 Heat the oil in a heavy-based pan or wok over a high heat. Add the onions and stir-fry for 3 minutes or until starting to soften but not brown. Add the ginger, garlic and chillies and continue stir-frying for 30 seconds, then reduce the heat to very low and leave to cook, stirring occasionally, until the onion is softened but nothing colours.

2 Stir in the turmeric, cumin, coriander, chilli powder and curry powder, and continue cooking very gently for a further 5 minutes. Don't burn the spices – sprinkle on a few drops of water if you're worried. Remove the pan from the heat and allow the mixture to cool a little.

3 Put 125ml of water in a food processor or blender and add the contents of the pan.

4 Blend until everything is smooth, then add the flour and blend again. Put the puréed mix back into the pan and simmer for 20–30 minutes (the longer the better in fact) over a very low heat, stirring occasionally. Add a little hot water if it starts to stick, but the idea is to gently 'fry' the sauce so that it darkens in colour to an orangey brown.

5 Once you have a thick paste, gradually stir in the stock and simmer, add in whichever vegetables you wish and allow them to cook while the sauce reduces and thickens, for 30 minutes or so. (If using meat or fish, cooking times can be adjusted accordingly.) Add in the onion seeds – they make it look authentic!

6 Serve with some rice, naan bread and chutney.

DUCK CROWN WITH POMEGRANATE SAUCE

Duck ... not the healthiest by any stretch of the imagination, but great for a treat meal. To remove the skin from the duck before cooking would be a crime against nature, DON'T DO IT! Enjoy the wonderful fatty, crispy skin and savour it, then be healthy for the rest of the week. Duck crown is the breast on the bone, which gives it maximum flavour, and can be bought in most supermarkets.

FEEDS 2

INGREDIENTS

1 duck crown
Sea salt and black pepper to season
1 shallot
Rapeseed oil
2 pomegranates
Squeeze of lemon juice
¼ of a vegetable stock cube
1 teaspoon cornflour

METHOD

1 Preheat the oven to 180°C.

2 Using a sharp knife, score the skin of the duck in criss-cross fashion, cutting down to the flesh but not into it. Season the skin with salt and pepper, rubbing it into the scores.

3 Heat a pan on a hot hob to smoking point, then place the duck on it, skin-side down and cook for 2–4 minutes getting colour all over and ensuring the skin crisps up. Turn it over and cook for a further 3 minutes before transferring to an oven dish and roasting, uncovered, for 20–25 minutes.

4 Peel and finely chop the shallot. Add some oil to a clean frying pan and fry the shallot gently until softened but not coloured. Cut the pomegranates in half and firmly squeeze out the juice into the pan, letting whatever seeds fall out remain there, then add a squeeze of lemon juice. Let the juice reduce by about half, then add in 200ml of hot water, crumble in the ¼ stock cube and stir until dissolved. Bring this to the boil.

5 In the meantime, combine the cornflour with a little water in a cup to make a thick paste. When the sauce in the pan is bubbling, add the paste and stir rapidly, reduce the heat and simmer until the sauce has thickened.

6 When the duck is cooked, remove onto a plate, cover with a sheet of foil and allow it to rest for at least 10 minutes before serving.

7 To serve, carefully cut the breast off the bone in two pieces or in slices, and pour the delicious sauce on the side.

FISHERMAN'S PIE

I made this fish pie a wee while ago when my brother and his family were down visiting. It really went down a treat. The hint of chilli in it gives it a lovely heat. This is quite an easy recipe, so even if you don't consider yourself a great cook I'm sure you will find this straightforward and very effective.

INGREDIENTS

FEEDS 4–6

1kg floury potatoes
300g salmon fillets, skinned and boned
300g smoked haddock or coley, skinned and boned
100g uncooked prawns, de-shelled and de-veined
1 large carrot
2 sticks of celery
Half a red chilli

Zest of 1 lemon
Knob of butter
Milk

For the sauce
600ml milk
2 tablespoons cornflour
2 tablespoons chopped chives
50g of low-fat cheese, grated
1–2 chicken/vegetable stock cubes, crumbled
1 tablespoon wholegrain mustard

METHOD

1 Place your peeled potatoes into a saucepan and just cover with cold water, then add a pinch of sea salt. Place the saucepan on the hob and turn on to a high heat and bring to the boil. Turn the heat down to medium for 10–15 minutes. Check the potatoes with a fork – if it stabs through easily they are done, if not leave them for a few more minutes until it does. Drain into a colander in the sink and let them stand for a few minutes. Place back into the saucepan and cover with a clean tea towel.

2 Cut all the fish into bite-sized chunks and mix with the prawns in a suitable-sized oven dish.

3 Coarsely grate the carrot and celery and finely grate the chilli and the zest of the lemon. Sprinkle all this over the top of the fish and toss roughly with your hands.

4 For the sauce, mix a little drop of the milk with the cornflour to make a paste. Put the remaining milk into a saucepan and heat gently. When warm add in the paste and stir, then add in the chives and half the cheese and crumble in the stock cube(s). Turn up the temperature and when the sauce is hot add in the mustard, then lower the heat again. Simmer until it is the consistency of double cream. Pour over the top of the fish and veg.

5 Mash the potatoes with some butter and milk until they are nice and creamy and cover the top of the pie with it. Sprinkle over the remaining grated cheese.

6 Pop the pie into a preheated oven at 200°C for 20 minutes or until the top has turned golden.

FRUITY OAT-CRUSTED CHICKEN

I think that if you have a good local butchers you should use it often. For certain things it may be a little more expensive than the supermarkets, but normally the quality of the meat will be better and a butcher is there to advise you on different cuts of meat and to do some of the work for you if you are a little unsure how to prepare a particular cut of meat. If you can afford it, I would suggest getting chicken fillets from your local butcher for this recipe. They will generally be plumper and definitely fresher.

The flesh of chicken fillets, when roasted in the oven, can go quite leathery and dry out quite easily, which is why they are normally wrapped in Parma ham or bacon, or coated in breadcrumbs, as this protective layer will help keep the breast moist during cooking. While this is a good thing, those options can be quite fatty, so this is my alternative ... a healthier approach to succulent chicken fillets with a flavoursome kick. Serve with some steamed or roasted vegetables.

FEEDS 2

INGREDIENTS

15g porridge oats
A sprig of rosemary leaves chopped
Zest of 1 orange
60ml fat-free natural yogurt
1 teaspoon wholegrain mustard
1 egg, beaten

30g plain flour
Sea salt and black pepper to season
2 large chicken fillets
2 teaspoons cranberry sauce
Olive oil

METHOD

1 Preheat the oven to 180°C.

2 In a medium bowl combine the oats, rosemary and orange zest. In another medium bowl beat together the yogurt, mustard and egg. Place the flour on a small plate and season with salt and pepper.

3 Place the chicken breasts on a chopping board and make a deep incision through the side of each breast to make deep pockets, being careful not to cut the whole way through. Delicately push a full teaspoon of cranberry sauce into each of these pockets and distribute it evenly. You can use a cocktail stick to 'stitch' the opening if you like – just remember to remove it after cooking!

4 Now roll a stuffed chicken fillet carefully in the seasoned flour, then into the yogurt mixture making sure that the coating has stuck to the flour, then finally roll it into the oats ensuring a good even coating of the oat mixture.

5 Lightly oil an oven tray and place the fillets on it, give them a very light drizzle of oil and bake for 35 minutes.

GNOCCHI AND COURGETTE RIBBONS WITH MASCARPONE

FEEDS 2

INGREDIENTS

300g gnocchi
1 red chilli
2 small courgettes
4 spring onions
Olive oil
Zest of 1 lemon
3 tablespoons mascarpone
50g Parmesan cheese, grated

I just adore gnocchi, they are so quick and handy and, like the humble spud, quite versatile. All that you need to do is add the gnocchi to a pot of boiling water and as soon as they rise to the surface they are cooked (normally within 2 minutes). Then you can do all sorts of things with them ... here is **one of my favourite recipes.**

METHOD

1 Cook the gnocchi according to the packet's instructions. When draining reserve half a cup of the cooking liquid.

2 De-seed and finely slice the chilli. Ribbon the courgettes by using a vegetable peeler and slice the spring onions on the diagonal. Put some oil in an ovenproof pan – it will be going under the grill later – and fry the chilli and courgettes over a medium/high heat until softened slightly. Add the spring onions, lemon zest, mascarpone, half the Parmesan cheese and the reserved cooking liquid. Stir in until you have a smooth sauce, then add the gnocchi. Stir to combine well.

3 Preheat the grill on a medium/high heat. Sprinkle the rest of the Parmesan cheese over the top of the gnocchi and place the pan under the grill (if you don't have an ovenproof pan, pour the mix into an ovenproof dish). Grill for a few minutes until bubbling.

4 Serve with dressed mixed salad leaves.

HEARTY LAMB STEW

FEEDS 6–8

The fragrance of this stew cooking around the house is enough to fill you with warmth on a cold, wet winter's day. I normally get it to the simmering stage and transfer it to the corner of my wood-burning stove and just let it bubble away for a few hours until the lamb falls apart ... heaven, served with a fresh crusty loaf!

INGREDIENTS

2 medium onions
4 cloves of garlic
Olive oil
2 carrots
2 parsnips
2 sticks of celery
2 heaped tablespoons plain flour
Sea salt and black pepper to season
500g diced stewing lamb
Glass of red wine
500ml vegetable stock
1 bouquet garni of fresh herbs
  (bay, mint, rosemary and thyme)

METHOD

1 If using an oven, preheat it to 180°C.

2 Peel and chop the onions and garlic and sweat in a casserole pan with 2 glugs of oil on a medium heat for 10 minutes.

3 Peel and chop the carrots and parsnips roughly. Trim the ends off the celery and chop it finely. Add all the vegetables into the casserole pan and sweat for 10 minutes.

4 In the meantime sprinkle the flour onto a large plate and season well with sea salt and fresh cracked black pepper. Pat the lamb pieces dry with kitchen paper and roll them in the seasoned flour.

5 Heat a frying pan and add a little oil. When hot, add a handful of the lamb to brown the meat, searing all sides. Do this in batches so that the meat browns rather than braises. Add the lamb to the casserole pan.

6 Add in the glass of wine to the casserole pan and turn up the heat until the liquid has reduced by at least half. Add in the stock and the bouquet of herbs. Bring to the boil, put the lid on and either simmer slowly on the hob or cook in an oven for at least 2½ hours.

7 Remove the bouquet garni before serving, check the seasoning and adjust if required. Serve with fresh crusty bread or creamy mash.

HONEY GLAZED HAM

A firm favourite at Christmas time, this is also an economical alternative to a roast dinner and leftovers can be used in all sorts of ways.

INGREDIENTS

2kg unsmoked boneless ham joint
1 carrot
1 onion
2 sticks of celery
1 teaspoon black peppercorns
1 teaspoon coriander seeds

2 bay leaves
Cloves for studding

For the glaze
200g demerara sugar
25ml white wine vinegar
100ml dry white wine
200g honey

FEEDS
6–8

METHOD

1 Place the ham into a large pot and cover with cold water. Peel and chop the carrot and onion and roughly chop the celery, then add these to the pot along with the black peppercorns, coriander seeds and bay leaves. Bring the pot to the boil, then reduce the heat to a simmer for 2½ hours. Skim off any impurities on the water surface and top up with water if needed during the cooking time. Carefully pour the cooking liquid away and allow the ham to cool slightly on a plate.

2 Preheat the oven to 180ºC. Place the ham in a suitable-sized roasting tin. Carefully cut away the skin leaving a thin layer of fat on the ham. Score the fat with a knife in a criss-cross pattern and stud each square with a clove.

3 To make the glaze, put the sugar, vinegar and wine into a pan and bring to the boil. Add the honey and bring to the boil again, then remove from the heat.

4 Pour half the glaze over the ham and roast in the oven for 15 minutes. Remove from the oven and pour the rest of the glaze over. Roast for a further 30–35 minutes, basting the juices over the top and turning the roasting tin a few times to get an even colour all over.

5 This ham can be made a day or two in advance of when you need it.

6 Serve with your favourite accompaniments.

ITALIAN COTTAGE PIE

FEEDS 4

This is my take on what I imagine an Italian version of cottage pie should be: good wholesome Italian flavours topped with the ultimate Italian comfort food ... gnocchi.

INGREDIENTS

1 medium onion

1 fat clove of garlic

Olive oil

140g pancetta or streaky bacon, diced

2 teaspoons dried oregano

500g lean lamb mince

200g chestnut mushrooms, chopped

100ml red wine

400g tin of chopped tomatoes

700g fresh gnocchi

50g Parmesan cheese

METHOD

1 Peel and finely chop the onion and garlic, then set aside.

2 Add a dash of oil to a large saucepan on a medium heat, fry the pancetta/bacon for a few minutes until starting to crisp up, then add in the oregano. Stir this around for a minute then add in the onion and garlic and cook gently until softened but not coloured.

3 Add the lamb mince to the saucepan and stir around until browned. Add in the chopped mushrooms and red wine, turn up the heat to full and bring to the boil. Add the chopped tomatoes, then half fill the tin with tap water and add it to the pot. Bring back to the boil and then reduce to a simmer. Keep simmering without a lid for 40–45 minutes, skimming off any froth that might appear on top.

4 With a few minutes of the cooking time left preheat the oven to 200°C.

5 Cook the gnocchi according to the packet's instructions, drain and set aside. Once the lamb is cooked, pour the saucepan contents into an ovenproof dish and top with the gnocchi. Grate over the Parmesan cheese and bake in the oven for 20 minutes until golden and bubbling.

OVEN-ROASTED LAMB CHOPS WITH THYME AND GARLIC

INGREDIENTS

1 bulb of garlic
Olive oil
3–4 sprigs of thyme
6–8 lamb chops
Sea salt and black pepper to season
Glass of white wine
Soy sauce
1 tablespoon honey

FEEDS 4

I love getting fresh lamb chops from my local butcher for this dish. Any type of chop will work well here for a very easy, flavoursome dinner.

METHOD

1 Preheat the oven to 180°C.

2 Put a frying pan on a hot hob and cut the garlic bulb in half and place on the pan cut side down along with a splash of oil and 2 sprigs of thyme. Season the chops with salt and pepper and put on the hot pan just to sear both sides. When all the chops are seared put them into a suitable-sized oven dish.

3 Keep the pan on the heat, pour in the glass of white wine and reduce by about half, stirring with a spatula, then add a good splash of soy sauce and the honey. Bring to the boil and then pour over the chops and place in the oven.

4 They should take 20–25 minutes, check halfway through and turn them over.

5 Serve with a fresh garnish of the remaining thyme and some steamed baby potatoes.

PORK AND APPLE STIR-FRY

Stir-fries are super quick to cook once the preparation work is out of the way.

INGREDIENTS

2 boneless pork chops
Sea salt and black pepper to season
1 medium onion
2 medium carrots
2 sticks of celery
1 red pepper
A thumb-sized piece of ginger
100ml cider
2 tablespoons dark soy sauce
1 teaspoon cornflour
Rapeseed oil
5 tablespoons apple sauce (shop-bought or home-made)

FEEDS 2

METHOD

1 Trim any excess fat from the pork chops and discard, then slice the pork into finger-thick strips and season with sea salt and black pepper.

2 Peel and slice the onion, slice the carrots and celery, de-seed the red pepper and slice it, and peel and finely dice the ginger.

3 In a small mixing bowl combine the cider and soy sauce, then whisk in the cornflour.

4 Heat a wok on a high heat and add a good glug of oil. When the oil is hot add the pork strips and stir-fry until no longer pink. Add in the prepared vegetables, stir-fry everything for a further 3–4 minutes before adding the apple sauce and the cornflour mix.

5 Cook for another 3–4 minutes until the sauce has thickened. Serve with some cooked rice or egg noodles.

PRAWN FRIED RICE

This dinner is a great home-made and healthy alternative to a Chinese takeaway. Please don't feel like it is only prawns that can be used ... all recipes can be altered to suit your own taste. You can use chicken, turkey, beef, pork or whatever else tickles your fancy. I just use a bag of small frozen prawns, which makes it really quick and easy.

INGREDIENTS

120g brown or wholegrain rice
A small head of broccoli
1 clove of garlic
1 large shallot
1 slice of cooked ham (optional)
Olive oil
250g bag of frozen prawns
1 medium egg
A handful of peas
2 tablespoons dark soy sauce

FEEDS 2

METHOD

1 Cook the rice according to the instructions on p. 222.

2 Cut the broccoli into small florets, peel and finely chop the shallot and garlic, and shred the ham (if using).

3 Add a little oil to a hot wok or large frying pan, add in the garlic and shallot and fry for a minute without colouring, then add in the prawns. Fry these for 2 minutes until coloured all over, then pick them out with tongs and set aside.

4 Add a little more oil to the pan and crack in the egg, move it around and break it up with a spatula until cooked, then add in the broccoli and peas. Fry all this for 3–4 minutes before adding in the cooked rice.

5 Continue stirring the contents of the pan/wok for a minute, then add in the soy sauce, ham (if using) and prawns, give this all a good mix around for another 2 minutes, then serve in warm bowls.

ROAST CHICKEN LEGS
WITH FIVE-SPICE SAUCE

The darker meat of a chicken, in my opinion, is the tastiest. In this recipe I leave the skin on as it crisps up really well in the oven and is mouth-watering. If you want to make it healthier just remove the skin before cooking.

Alternatively this recipe can be made with a full chicken that has been jointed. Jointing a chicken is something you can practice yourself or simply ask your butcher to do for you.

There is a little bit of work involved in the sauce, although I feel it is worth it — it has a beautiful flavour and creamy texture and it fills the room with its wonderful aroma.

INGREDIENTS

4 chicken legs – jointed
1 teaspoon Chinese five-spice
Sea salt and black pepper to season
1 lemon
1 bulb of garlic
A few sprigs of thyme
Olive oil

For the sauce

1 small onion
1 medium carrot
6–7 cherry tomatoes
1 tablespoon toasted sesame oil
50ml white wine vinegar
400ml chicken stock
A bouquet garni (rosemary, thyme and bay)
100ml double cream
1 teaspoon Chinese five-spice

FEEDS 4

METHOD

1 Preheat the oven to maximum temperature (usually about 250°C). Carefully joint the chicken legs with a large heavy, sharp knife to make a drumstick and a thigh. Place the chicken pieces in a suitable-sized oven dish and sprinkle lightly with the five-spice and some salt and pepper.

2 Quarter or slice the lemon and add to the dish with the garlic, separated into peeled cloves, and sprigs of thyme. Drizzle with a little olive oil, place in the oven and keep at full temperature for ten minutes, then turn down to 200°C for 50 minutes.

To make the sauce

1 Chop the onion and carrot and cut the cherry tomatoes in half. Put a sauce-pan onto a hot hob and add the sesame oil, then the onion and carrot and sweat for 2 minutes. Remove from the heat and add the vinegar and leave for 1 minute. Then return to the heat, add the chicken stock, tomatoes and the bouquet garni and bring to the boil. Reduce the heat to a steady simmer.

2 Remove from the heat when the sauce has thickened and coats the back of a spoon. Add the cream and five-spice and put back onto the heat and gently bubble for a few minutes.

3 Serve over the chicken right away, or keep warm until you are ready.

ROAST LEG OF LAMB STAB-STUFFED WITH GARLIC, ROSEMARY AND ANCHOVIES

INGREDIENTS

2.5kg leg of lamb
2 large onions
2 carrots
2 sticks of celery
50g tin of drained anchovies
7–8 cloves of garlic
Few sprigs of rosemary
Olive oil

FEEDS 4

Lamb is my meat of choice right now. The flavour that comes from a leg roasted like this is second to none! Rosemary and garlic are classic flavours with lamb, but the addition of the anchovy just brings an extra sweetness and salty spike. This is terrific with my home-made mint sauce (p. 279).

METHOD

1 Remove the leg of lamb from the fridge half an hour before you start.

2 Preheat the oven to 180°C. Peel and cut the onion into thick wedges and roughly chop the carrots and celery and set aside.

3 Pat dry an anchovy fillet and wrap it around a peeled, halved garlic clove and a cut piece of rosemary, then stab the lamb and push it into the hole. Do this all over, about fifteen times.

4 Drizzle over a little oil and season well, place in a roasting tray with the vegetables and bung it into the oven for 1–1¼ hours, basting the juices over the top once or twice during cooking, until the meat is tender.

5 Let it rest out of the oven for 15–20 minutes before carving. There is no real technique to carving – I stand it up holding the bone and cut off thin slices. Serve with your favourite side dishes.

RUSTIC ROAST CHICKEN, CHUNKY CROUTON AND ROASTED CHERRY TOMATO SALAD

INGREDIENTS

1 medium chicken
Olive oil
1 lemon
A small bunch of thyme
1 bulb of garlic
1 teaspoon Chinese five-spice
Sea salt and black pepper to season

400g cherry tomatoes
1 crusty loaf
6 rashers of smoky bacon
Cider vinegar
1 tablespoon wholegrain mustard
A bunch of soft herbs (basil, mint, parsley)
6 spring onions

FEEDS 4–6

METHOD

1 Take your bird out of the fridge half an hour before you need it to bring it up to room temperature.

2 Preheat the oven as high as it will go (usually about 250ºC). Place the chicken in an oiled oven tray and cut the string that ties it so that it 'relaxes'. Prick the lemon all over with a knife and stuff it into the cavity along with the thyme, three peeled cloves of garlic and the five-spice. Drizzle the outside with oil and rub with salt and pepper.

3 Pop the chicken in the oven. Keep it up at maximum heat for 15 minutes, then turn it down to 190ºC for 1 hour 10 minutes, basting the bird a few times with the juices in the pan.

4 In the meantime cut all the cherry tomatoes in half and peel the rest of the cloves of garlic. Twenty minutes before the chicken is due to be ready, remove it from the oven, lift it out of the tray and scatter in the tomatoes and garlic. Then pop the bird back on top and place back into the oven until cooked – when the leg joint is pierced with a fork the juices should run clear.

5 Transfer the chicken to a plate and allow to rest and cool. Tear the crusty loaf into large bite-sized pieces and put them into the roasting tray, toss them around with the tomatoes and garlic, then spread them in an even layer and cut up the bacon and scatter on top.

6 Place back into the oven for around 20 minutes until golden and crispy.

7 Meanwhile remove all the skin from the chicken and use two forks to shred all the meat possible from the bone. Pile it into a large bowl and spoon in any of the resting juices from the plate. Drizzle some good olive oil over, a good splash of cider vinegar and the wholegrain mustard, and give it a good mix around. Chop up the herb leaves and finely slice the spring onions and add them to the bowl, giving everything a light toss again, then taste and season further if needed.

8 Once the croutons are golden and crisp, toss everything together and tip it onto a large platter in the middle of the table for everyone to help themselves.

9 Serve with some steamed greens if you like – broccoli, green beans or whatever appeals to you.

SAUSAGE ONE-DISH WONDER

You know those evenings when no matter how much you enjoy cooking you just couldn't be bothered? We have all had them! Well, this dish is for exactly those evenings. It is fuss free, everything is chucked into one dish and bunged into the oven for about 30 minutes.

INGREDIENTS

8–10 baby potatoes
8 good quality sausages
1 large pepper
3 cloves of garlic
Rapeseed oil
A punnet of cherry tomatoes
3 sprigs of rosemary
Sea salt and black pepper to season

FEEDS 4

METHOD

1 Preheat the oven to 200°C.

2 Quarter the baby potatoes, separate the sausages, de-seed and slice the pepper and peel the garlic cloves.

3 Drizzle a little oil into a large roasting tray and add all the ingredients including the tomatoes and rosemary, drizzle another little bit of oil over the top, season with salt and pepper and toss the ingredients around. Roast in the oven for 30–35 minutes.

4 Divide between four plates to serve.

SMOKED HADDOCK LASAGNE

INGREDIENTS

200g smoked haddock fillets

50g low-fat cheese

600ml skimmed milk

2 tablespoons cornflour

A small bunch of fresh chives, chopped

1–2 fish/chicken stock cubes

2 teaspoons wholegrain mustard

2 handfuls of frozen sweetcorn

Pasta sheets (fresh or dried)

FEEDS 2

When you hear 'Lasagne' you automatically think of the traditional Bolognese one, but there are so many variations you can experiment with. This dish has become a firm favourite in my house because it is very tasty and it is low fat. Smoked coley works just as well as haddock and is generally cheaper. Just make sure all the bones are removed from the fish.

METHOD

1 Preheat the oven to 200°C. Skin the smoked haddock fillets and cut into chunks.

2 Grate the cheese and set aside.

3 Blend a little drop of the milk with the cornflour to make a paste. Put the remaining milk into a saucepan and heat gently. When warm add in the paste and stir, add in the chives and half the cheese and crumble in the stock cube(s). Bring up the heat until it starts to bubble. Then, and only then, add the wholegrain mustard, otherwise the sauce will separate. Bring it back down to a gentle simmer until it has the consistency of double cream.

4 Put a layer of half the haddock and a small handful of sweetcorn in a lasagne dish, pour just over a third of the sauce over, season well and top with pasta sheets. Repeat this again and pour the remainder of sauce on the top layer and sprinkle with the other half of the grated cheese.

5 Bung into oven for 30 minutes, then serve with a salad. It's just that simple!

SPANISH SEAFOOD RICE

INGREDIENTS

1 large onion
2 cloves of garlic
1 red pepper
1 green pepper
Olive oil
200g paella rice or Arborio rice
800ml fish or vegetable stock
A pinch of saffron
400g seafood mix
2 lemons
A small bunch of parsley to garnish

FEEDS 4

This is called Spanish Seafood Rice as opposed to Paella as it is a much-simplified version of a traditional paella. I use a frozen seafood mix here that has been defrosted slowly in the fridge.

METHOD

1 Peel and finely chop the onion, peel and mince or finely chop the garlic, and de-seed and slice the peppers.

2 Heat some oil in a large pan over a medium/high heat, add the onion and garlic and cook gently until softened but not coloured for about 5 minutes. Add in the peppers and cook for a further 3 minutes. Add the rice and stir it around for 2 minutes before adding the stock. Then add the saffron and bring to the boil. Reduce to a simmer and stir occasionally as the rice absorbs the stock.

3 When the stock is all absorbed and the rice is plump and tender, add the seafood mix and the juice from half a lemon, and cook for a further 3–4 minutes until everything is completely cooked. Serve in warm bowls with wedges of the remaining lemon and some chopped parsley scattered over.

SPICE CRUSTED ROAST BEEF

FEEDS 4–6

Roast beef makes a truly wonderful Sunday roast. There are several different joints you can get and it all depends on your taste or, more importantly, your budget. Ask your local butcher for advice on this and please remember that more expensive doesn't necessarily mean more flavoursome.

This is a lovely way to bring a little heat to roast beef. Your lips will be tingling after it; the crust also protects the meat from drying out. Home-made Yorkshire puddings (p. 231) are great with this.

INGREDIENTS

1.5kg roasting joint (of your choice)
1 small onion
1 carrot
2 sticks of celery
Small bunch of rosemary
Small bunch of thyme
1 bulb of garlic
Olive oil
1 tablespoon sea salt
2 tablespoons black peppercorns
2 tablespoons caraway seeds
1 tablespoon cloves
5 tablespoons red wine vinegar
2 tablespoons honey

METHOD

1 Take the beef joint out of the fridge about half an hour before you plan to start cooking to bring it up to room temperature.

2 Preheat the oven to its maximum temperature (usually around 250°C).

3 Chop the vegetables roughly – no need to peel them as they are for flavour only. Toss them into a suitable-sized roasting tray along with the herbs and the garlic separated into cloves. Drizzle with oil.

4 Drizzle oil over the roasting joint and rub it all over.

5 In a pestle and mortar crush the salt, peppercorns, caraway seeds and cloves together and pour the mixture out onto a plate. Roll the beef in the spices coating it all over evenly and then seal the joint all over in a hot pan. Place it on top of the prepared vegetables in the roasting tray.

6 With the pan still on the heat, pour in the red wine vinegar and honey. Stir around to incorporate any tasty bits stuck to the pan and boil until reduced by half. Pour the reduction over the beef in the roasting tray.

7 Place the tray in the hot oven and turn the heat down to 200°C. Roast for 1 hour for medium beef. If you prefer it a little rarer or a little more well done give or take 10–15 minutes accordingly. Take it out of the oven halfway through the cooking time and baste it with the juices in the tray.

8 When it is cooked to your liking, remove from the roasting tray and place on a clean chopping board, cover with tinfoil and a clean tea towel and allow to rest for 20 minutes before carving.

9 Remove the string and with a long, sharp carving knife cut in thin, clean slices, holding it in place with a fork. Serve with your favourite side dishes.

STUFFED PORK CHOPS WITH SAGE

FEEDS 4

This is my take on quite a regular weekly dinner. This version really increases the flavour and will leave you wanting more.

INGREDIENTS

1kg floury potatoes, cut in 2cm/1in diced pieces with the skins left on

4 thick pork chops on the bone

50g softened butter

4 dried apricots, finely diced

1 bulb of garlic

16 fresh sage leaves

Sea salt and black pepper to season

Rapeseed oil

Plain flour

200g packet of bacon lardons

METHOD

1 Preheat the oven to 220°C.

2 Put the potatoes into a saucepan of salted water and bring to the boil. Boil for 4–5 minutes as you only need to parboil them. Drain them in a colander and let them steam dry.

3 Lay the pork chops flat on a chopping board and insert a small paring knife horizontally into the chop and make a hidden pocket, making sure the tip of the knife does not come out either side.

4 Mash together the butter, dried apricots, a peeled and finely chopped clove of garlic, 8 chopped sage leaves and a pinch of both salt and pepper. Push this flavoured butter into the pockets of the pork chops, dividing it up evenly.

5 Take 8 more leaves of sage and toss them in oil, then dip one side in some plain flour and stick one, flour side down onto each side of the chops. Set aside.

6 Pour the potatoes into a large ovenproof dish along with the bacon lardons and the rest of the cloves of garlic, peeled. Season and drizzle with oil and place into the preheated oven for 30–35 minutes altogether.

7 When the potatoes have been in the oven for 10 minutes place a frying pan on a hot hob and add a drizzle of oil. When the pan is really hot put in the chops and fry for 10 minutes turning occasionally to get them nice and golden.

8 Remove the dish from the oven, add the chops on top, and pop back into the oven for the final 10–15 minutes depending on the thickness of the chops.

SWEET AND SOUR PORK

There is a nice heat from the chilli and ginger in this recipe, which isn't the norm for a sweet and sour recipe, but it gives it a kick that I think it needs. This is a very quick recipe, so get cooking the rice according to the packet instructions (or see pp. 222–3 for more interesting variations) before you start frying. Have all the ingredients chopped and ready to go before you start cooking.

FEEDS 2

INGREDIENTS

200g pork fillet
Sea salt and black pepper to season
1 onion
1 red pepper
1 yellow pepper
1 fat clove of garlic, peeled
½ small red chilli
A thumb-sized piece of ginger, peeled

Rapeseed oil
1 teaspoon of Chinese five-spice
1 tablespoon cornflour
3 tablespoons dark soy sauce
A small tin of pineapple chunks in juice
2 tablespoons balsamic vinegar
Coriander leaves to garnish

METHOD

1 Cut the pork fillet lengthways down the middle, then cut each side into chunks and season with salt and pepper.

2 Peel and halve the onion and chop it into chunks. De-seed the peppers and chop them into bite-sized pieces. Finely slice the garlic, chilli and ginger.

3 Set a large frying pan or wok over a high heat and when hot add some oil and the pork pieces. Immediately sprinkle over the five-spice and brown the pork for a few minutes. Remove to a clean bowl using a slotted spoon.

4 Give the pan/wok a wipe down with kitchen roll, then return to the heat, add more oil, then add the onion, peppers, chilli, ginger and garlic. Cook these for about two minutes, stirring frequently.

5 Stir in the cornflour and add the soy sauce, then cook for a further minute.

6 Add the pork back in along with the pineapple chunks, their juice and the balsamic vinegar.

7 Check the seasoning and cook for a further few minutes ensuring the pork is cooked through (break a piece open to check). Simmer for a few minutes until the sauce thickens, if needed.

8 Serve with rice and a garnish of coriander leaves.

THIRTY-GARLIC-CLOVE CHICKEN CASSEROLE

INGREDIENTS

4 chicken legs
Olive oil
2 medium red onions
2 tablespoons plain flour
200ml dry white wine
200ml chicken stock
2 teaspoons Dijon mustard
Sea salt and black pepper to season
3 bulbs of garlic
A small bunch of thyme

FEEDS 4

I know thirty cloves of garlic might seem excessive, but once you taste this you will understand. Plus the health benefits from the garlic alone are worth it. This is a fantastic casserole to make if you are feeling under the weather.

METHOD

1 Preheat the oven to 200°C.

2 Divide the chicken legs into two pieces by cutting between the thigh and drumstick with a sharp, heavy knife. Get a large frying pan nice and hot and heat some oil. Brown the chicken in batches, adding it to a large casserole dish when browned.

3 Add a little more oil to the pan and heat again, peel and quarter the red onions and fry in the pan until slightly coloured all over, add in the flour and gradually stir in the wine and stock until smooth. Add the mustard and season with salt and pepper. Allow this sauce to simmer for 5 minutes.

4 Break up the garlic bulbs, count out thirty cloves and add them to the casserole dish – there is no need to peel them. Add in the thyme, then pour the sauce carefully over the chicken in the casserole dish.

5 Place in the oven with the lid on and cook for 1½ hours.

6 Serve with some creamy mashed potatoes for the ultimate 'feel good' meal.

TIP: I don't use the traditional white sauce as I find it a bit heavy – I use low-fat crème fraiche instead. You can buy lasagne sheets in any supermarket or alternatively make your own pasta (see p. 281) – it's easy and rewarding.

TRADITIONAL LASAGNE OR SPAGHETTI BOLOGNESE

INGREDIENTS

FEEDS 4–6

2 rashers of smoked streaky bacon
1 large onion
2 carrots
2 cloves of garlic
2 sticks of celery
Olive oil
1 heaped tablespoon dried oregano
250g minced beef

250g minced pork
2 tins of chopped, peeled tomatoes
3 tablespoons tomato purée
1 tablespoon anchovy paste (optional)
Sea salt and black pepper to season
2 tablespoons Worcestershire sauce
150g Parmesan cheese
500ml tub of low-fat crème fraiche
250g dried lasagne sheets

METHOD

1 Finely chop the bacon. Peel and finely chop the onion, carrots and garlic, and chop the celery, then set aside.

2 Place a large pan on a high heat and add a good splash of oil, the bacon and the oregano. Fry until the bacon is colouring slightly. Add in the chopped onion, celery, carrots and garlic, and stir once every minute for about 7–8 minutes.

3 Add in the two minces along with the tinned tomatoes, then fill one tin with water and pour it in also. Add in the tomato purée and the anchovy paste (if using), then season well and bring to the boil. Turn down the heat and simmer with the lid on for around 45 minutes. While the sauce is simmering, stir in the Worcestershire sauce.

4 Preheat the oven to 190ºC.

5 Remove the sauce from the heat and grate in about a quarter of the Parmesan cheese and stir it in, have a quick taste and season a little more if required. At this point the sauce can be used for Spaghetti Bolognese or allowed to cool down fully, then frozen in batches.

6 For Lasagne: Spoon a layer of about a third of the sauce into an ovenproof dish. Place a single layer of pasta sheets on top and spread a third of the crème fraiche over them. Season, then grate another quarter of the Parmesan cheese over this.

7 Repeat the step above twice more, finishing with a layer of grated Parmesan cheese on top.

8 Cover with foil and bung into the oven for about 20 minutes. Remove the foil and cook for a further 25–30 minutes until golden and bubbling.

9 Serve the lasagne with a fresh side salad.

TURKEY AND LEEK PIE

I came up with this pie to use up leftover turkey at Christmas. I had big juicy fat leeks in my garden all over the hard winter and I made a sauce from what I had in the fridge. It worked. In fact, it worked very well indeed! It is a great way of using up leftovers (if you are using leftovers, simply tear the turkey into strips or cut into bite-sized pieces and add to the pie), but I now buy turkey fillets in the supermarket specifically to make this. Turkey is such a lean meat (the leanest of all) and I use it a lot to make healthy dinners.

INGREDIENTS

FEEDS 4

1 fresh turkey fillet, roughly 750g
2–3 rashers of smoked streaky bacon
Knob of butter
3 trimmed and washed leeks
2 cloves of garlic
Sea salt and black pepper to season

Juice of half a lemon
200g cream cheese
150ml milk
2 tablespoons wholegrain mustard
Half a nutmeg
One batch of flaky pastry (see p. 278)
1 medium egg

METHOD

1 Preheat the oven to 190°C. Cut the turkey into bite-sized cubes and set aside.

2 Cut up the bacon and add to a saucepan with the melted butter. Fry off for a few minutes until coloured and crispy.

3 Slice the leeks, peel and finely chop the garlic and add them to the bacon in the saucepan. Sweat these for about 10 minutes over a medium heat, stirring occasionally to prevent them from sticking.

4 Season the turkey pieces with salt and pepper and add them to the saucepan, brown them and then squeeze in the juice of half a lemon. Season everything with a little salt and pepper.

5 Stir in the cream cheese and milk, bring to the brink of a boil, add the mustard, grate the nutmeg over and give another good stir to mix the flavours.

6 Reduce the heat to a simmer. Let this mixture simmer for 5–10 minutes to thicken the sauce (add more milk if the sauce is getting too thick), check the taste and season if required. Take off the heat and pour into a suitable-sized oven dish.

7 Roll out the pastry slightly bigger than the size of the oven dish. Lay it over the top and tuck the sides in. If a side is too big just cut it off. Stab the pastry a few times with a knife to let the steam out. Whisk up an egg and brush it over the pastry.

8 Bake in the oven for 25–30 minutes until the pastry is golden. Serve with a green salad.

WHOLE FISH BAKED IN A FOIL PARCEL

FEEDS 1

INGREDIENTS

Soft butter
Sea salt and black pepper to season
1 small onion
1 whole fish of your choice
A few sprigs of thyme
A few bay leaves
1 clove of garlic, bashed
1 small fennel bulb
1 lemon

Watching the likes of *River Cottage* really has me trying every kind of fish I can either buy or catch myself. This dish can be made with sea bass, sea trout, brown trout or sea bream. You can get your fishmonger to scale and gut it for you, if it has not already been done, but usually it will be prepared already. Don't ever be afraid to ask your fishmonger to prepare something the way you need it or even for advice on how to cook it. It's part of their job and they are usually very helpful.

METHOD

1 Preheat the oven to 200ºC.

2 Tear off two squares of tinfoil and lie on top of each other. Smear the dull side of the top one with a little softened butter, sprinkle on salt and pepper and some slices of onion.

3 Pat the fish dry and place it on top of the onions. Smear a little butter over the top of the fish and season it. Stuff the thyme, bay leaves, some more butter and the bashed garlic clove into the cavity.

4 Slice the fennel bulb and throw some slices over and around the fish and squeeze half a lemon over everything.

5 Scrunch the edges of the foil together to seal the parcel and set it on a baking tray. Bung it into the hot oven and bake for 20 minutes.

6 Remove from the oven and check with a sharp knife to make certain it is cooked right through. Poke the thickest part: it should all be white and coming away from the bone. If it is not, another few minutes in the oven should do it.

7 Serve with boiled new potatoes and steamed vegetables. Just fork the flesh off the bones as you eat, and be careful not to swallow any bones!

SIDES

BRAISED RED CABBAGE AND BRAMLEY APPLE IN CIDER VINEGAR

FEEDS 4

This is a gorgeous accompaniment to any pork dish. It is sweet but has a nice sharpness from the cider vinegar that really works. It doesn't just look pretty but tastes top class too.

INGREDIENTS

1 small red cabbage
1 Bramley apple
150g butter
150ml cider vinegar
150g light brown sugar
1 cinnamon stick
Pinch of ground cloves
Sea salt and black pepper to season

METHOD

1 Preheat the oven to 180ºC.

2 Cut the cabbage into quarters, core and finely shred it. Peel and core the Bramley apple and slice it finely.

3 Put the butter, vinegar and sugar into an ovenproof saucepan over a medium heat and dissolve the sugar. Add in the cinnamon and cloves and season with salt and pepper.

4 Toss in the cabbage and apple, coating it all.

5 Place the lid on the saucepan or cover with wet, crumpled greaseproof paper and bung it the oven. Bake for about an hour, stirring occasionally, until the cabbage is tender and the apple has all but dissolved.

6 Lift off the lid or paper and bake for a further 10–15 minutes so the remaining liquid reduces to a nice glossy syrup.

BROCCOLI AND LEEK BAKE

One day I was making creamy leeks but decided I wanted a bit more texture, and this was the result. This dish works well with chicken or lamb but can be served with any type of roast meat. I think breadcrumbs are something that everyone should have to hand. We all have times where bread has gone hard on us, especially crusty loaves or baguettes, so instead of turfing them out why not blitz them up and freeze them.

FEEDS 4

INGREDIENTS

1 head of broccoli
2 large leeks
2 shallots
50g butter
50g flour
175ml semi-skimmed milk
100g low-fat cheddar cheese, grated
Half a nutmeg
A vegetable stockpot/cube
Large handful of breadcrumbs
100g Parmesan cheese, grated

METHOD

1 Preheat the oven to 200°C.

2 Cut the broccoli into small pieces and steam or parboil it. Cut and wash the leeks, then slice thinly.

3 Finely chop the shallots and add them with the butter to a pan on a medium/high heat, sauté for a few minutes, then stir in the flour. Once the flour is absorbed, add the leeks and sauté for another few minutes until softened.

4 Stir in the milk, a little at a time, over a low heat until you have a creamy consistency, add in the grated cheddar and stir until dissolved. Grate in the nutmeg and add the stockpot or crumble in the stock cube. Again stir until dissolved.

5 Add the broccoli, give it all a good stir, then transfer it to a suitable-sized oven dish. Level out the contents and add a layer of breadcrumbs topped with the grated Parmesan cheese. Place in the preheated oven and bake for 25 minutes until golden and crunchy on top and bubbling around the edges.

HASSELBACK POTATOES

FEEDS 4

INGREDIENTS

500g baby potatoes
Few sprigs of rosemary
Olive oil
Sea salt and black pepper to season

There is a little bit to do in the preparation of this dish, but the results are well worth it. I think they look great and give a 'wow' factor to any meal, and the flavours will speak for themselves.

METHOD

1   Preheat the oven to 200ºC.

2   Wash the potatoes and finely chop the rosemary leaves.

3   Slice the potatoes (leaving the skins on) width ways only a few millimetres apart, but not cutting the whole way through. (The way I do this is put a coaster (see picture) either side of the potato and slice down until the knife hits the coaster.)

4   When sliced, fan out the potatoes, just spreading the slices apart so they open up, and place in an oven dish. Drizzle with some oil and sprinkle over the chopped rosemary and some sea salt and black pepper, ensuring some gets down in between the slices.

5   Roast in the oven for about 45 minutes until golden and crispy on the outside.

MINTED MUSHY PEAS

This is a super and fast way to jazz up some regular frozen peas.

INGREDIENTS   FEEDS 2

A knob of butter
180g of frozen peas
A large sprig of mint

Lemon juice
Sea salt and black pepper to season

METHOD

1 Melt the butter in a saucepan over a medium/high heat and add in the peas.

2 Finely chop the leaves from the sprig of mint and add them to the saucepan, give it a good stir, then pop a lid on the saucepan and allow to heat through for 10 minutes.

3 Add a good squeeze of lemon juice along with a pinch of salt and a generous pinch of black pepper to flavour. Give it a good mash up with a potato masher until thick and creamy.

SEARED CORN ON THE COB IN HONEY AND BALSAMIC VINEGAR

This is a simple way to inject some flavour and style to a simple vegetable. It gives it a sticky sweet and charred flavour as though the corn had come off a BBQ.

INGREDIENTS   FEEDS 2

2 large fresh corn on the cob
2 tablespoons honey
2 tablespoons balsamic vinegar

METHOD

1 Cut the cobs carefully into four equal pieces with a heavy, sharp knife, then place in a large saucepan of cold, salted water. Bring to the boil, then simmer for 2 minutes.

2 Drain in a colander and steam dry for 2 minutes.

3 Heat a pan or preferably a griddle pan and place the corn on it. Then drizzle over both the honey and balsamic vinegar and give it all a good shake around.

4 Fry them for about 5 minutes on a high temperature, moving them around to get coloured all over.

MY 'HOLY TRINITY' GRAVY

Now just in case anyone thinks that The Father, Son and Holy Spirit came up with this — they didn't; they only wish they had! What I mean by 'Holy Trinity' is the three sauces I add to my gravy to make it blow your socks off. This technique works for any roast dinner so give it a try next Sunday. Any roast dish you make, always throw some vegetables in under and around the roast — these are not to eat but to help keep the roast moist and for flavour, then when the roast is done they are used for the gravy. Give this method a go ... it is consistently amazing!

INGREDIENTS   FEEDS 4–6

1 tablespoon flour

A glass of wine, red or white

1 litre of vegetable, chicken or beef stock

Black pepper to season

Knob of butter

The Holy Trinity

1 tablespoon dark soy sauce

1 tablespoon oyster sauce

1 tablespoon Worcestershire sauce

METHOD

1   Once you take your roast out and leave it to rest, spoon off the fat from the roasting dish, then sprinkle the flour over the vegetables in the tray. Mash them all together with a potato masher and stir well.

2   Pour in the wine of your choice and bung back into the hot oven (or if your tray is hob proof, place it on a hot hob). Let the wine reduce, then add your hot stock and allow to bubble for a little while.

3   Carefully sieve the contents of the tray into a saucepan and place onto a hot hob, bring to the boil and add in 'The Holy Trinity'. Reduce to a steady simmer until it thickens, season with black pepper; the soy sauce should be salty enough.

4   When ready to serve up, take it off the heat, add a knob of butter and stir to dissolve: this will make it nice and shiny and silky smooth. Serve it up in a nice big gravy boat; you won't have a drop left!

TIP: If you have no wine to hand then use your imagination ... cider, port, sherry, apple juice, orange juice, etc., anything like this will do and if worse comes to worst just use the stock and add a squeeze of lemon juice.

PAN-FRIED POTATOES
WITH GARLIC AND ROSEMARY

These bad boys are so fragrant and tasty they nearly become the main feature in many meals. They will go with any meat and I eat them once or twice every week. I could honestly eat them every day they are so gorgeous. Give them a go and jazz up the humble spud!

FEEDS 4

INGREDIENTS

1kg baby potatoes
1 teaspoon sea salt
1 fat clove of garlic
1 sprig of rosemary
Olive oil

METHOD

1 Scrub the baby potatoes and cut them into quarters (unpeeled). Place them into a saucepan of salted water and put on a high heat. Bring to the boil, then turn down the heat and cook for 5 minutes or until you can push a fork into them. Drain in a colander in the sink and let them steam dry for a few minutes.

2 Put the sea salt and peeled garlic clove in a pestle and mortar and grind into a paste. Strip the rosemary and finely chop the leaves, add it to the paste and pour in a good glug of oil and mix all around.

3 Pour this mixture into a large frying pan on the hob on a medium heat so as not to burn the paste, then pour in the parboiled potatoes and turn up the heat slightly.

4 Toss the potatoes around, ensuring they all get coated with the mixture.

5 Shake them every now and again over a medium/high heat for 20–25 minutes until coloured and crispy on the outside and fluffy on the inside.

POTATO, GARLIC AND CHIVE MASH

Roasted garlic is sweet and full of flavour; this is the perfect mash to accompany any meal.

INGREDIENTS

FEEDS 4

1 medium bulb of garlic
Olive oil
800g floury potatoes
150ml whole milk
A knob of butter
Sea salt and black pepper to season
A small bunch of snipped chives

METHOD

1 Preheat the oven to 180°C.

2 Set the garlic bulb on a sheet of tinfoil, drizzle with oil, then wrap it up in the foil and roast in the oven for 1 hour.

3 Peel and cut the potatoes into large, even-sized chunks. Place them in a large saucepan, cover with cold water and add a pinch of salt. Bring the saucepan to the boil on a hot hob and cook for a further 15 minutes until the potatoes can be pierced with a fork. Drain them into a colander in the sink and place back into the saucepan, cover the top of the saucepan with a clean tea towel and put the lid back on. Allow them to steam dry off the heat for 5–10 minutes so they fluff up.

4 Gently heat the milk and butter in a small saucepan.

5 Mash the potatoes in their saucepan with some seasoning, then pour in the warmed milk. Mash thoroughly until lump free.

6 Cut the garlic bulb in half and squeeze out the lovely fragrant soft garlic flesh into the potatoes. Rapidly stir this into the potatoes and transfer to a serving dish, then top with some fresh chopped chives.

POTATO, LEEK AND MUSTARD MASH

I do like to experiment with mashed potatoes as, fine and all as they are, sometimes new and fresh ideas can turn a good meal into a great meal.

FEEDS 4

INGREDIENTS

800g floury potatoes
2 young leeks
Olive oil
150ml whole milk
A knob of butter
Sea salt and black pepper to season
1 tablespoon wholegrain mustard

METHOD

1 Peel and cut the potatoes into large even-sized chunks. Place them in a large saucepan, cover with cold water and add a pinch of salt. Bring the saucepan to the boil on a hot hob and cook for a further 15 minutes until the potatoes can be pierced with a fork. Drain them into a colander in the sink and place back into the saucepan, cover the top of the saucepan with a clean tea towel and put the lid back on. Allow them to steam dry off the heat for 5–10 minutes so they fluff up.

2 In the meantime wash, trim and slice the leeks into 1cm/½in slices. Add a little oil to a pan on a medium heat and gently fry the leeks until just about softened.

3 Drain them onto some kitchen paper.

4 Gently heat the milk and butter in a small saucepan. Mash the potatoes in their saucepan with some seasoning, then pour in the warmed milk. Mash this thoroughly until lump free.

5 Add in the leeks and mustard and stir rapidly with a wooden spoon until well combined and you have fluffy creamy potatoes.

POTATO, PARSNIP AND NUTMEG MASH

The sweetness of the parsnips really breaks through here, along with that fragrant oomph from the nutmeg. Ground nutmeg is fine, but to get the great flavour punch it is best to grate a whole nut with a micro grater.

FEEDS 4

INGREDIENTS

800g floury potatoes
3–4 parsnips
150ml whole milk
A knob of butter
Sea salt and black pepper to season
Half a nutmeg

METHOD

1 Peel and cut the potatoes into large even-sized chunks. Peel and cut the parsnips into similar chunks and place both into a large saucepan, cover with cold water and add a pinch of salt. Bring the saucepan to the boil on a hot hob and cook for a further 15 minutes until the potatoes can be pierced with a fork.

2 Drain them and place back into the saucepan, off the heat, cover the top of the saucepan with a clean tea towel and firm the lid back on to allow to steam dry for 5–10 minutes so they fluff up.

3 Gently heat the milk and butter in a small saucepan. Mash the potatoes and parsnips in their saucepan with a generous pinch of sea salt, black pepper and the grated nutmeg, then pour in the warmed milk. Mash this thoroughly until lump free.

4 Stir rapidly with a wooden spoon and transfer to a serving dish, top with some extra grated nutmeg.

RED ONION GRAVY

This is a sweet gravy that will go with any roast meat. It also freezes well if you have managed to keep some over.

FEEDS 4

INGREDIENTS

4 red onions
Olive oil
5 tablespoons balsamic vinegar
Knob of butter
Sea salt and black pepper to season
400ml chicken or vegetable stock

METHOD

1 Finely slice the onions and put them into a saucepan with a tablespoon of oil on a medium heat. Sweat the onions for about 15 minutes.

2 Turn up the heat to full and when hot add the balsamic vinegar and stir until it has evaporated. Turn the heat back down again and add the butter. Season well with sea salt and black pepper.

3 Add the stock to the onions. Bring to a simmer for 10 minutes – then it's ready to serve.

TIP: If you are not too confident on your knife skills I would suggest purchasing a mandolin. They are fast and convenient but very, very sharp, so watch the fingers! However, if you are serious about cooking, stick with the knife ... speed and skills will come through practice.

RICE THREE WAYS

This is a foolproof way to get fluffy, non-stodgy rice. The addition of the spices and other ingredients are just to get the taste buds twitching.

METHOD

1 Measure out one cup of white rice and pour into a medium/large saucepan. Measure 1½ cups of cold water, pour into the saucepan and throw in a pinch of salt. Place the saucepan on a high heat and bring to the boil, reduce the temperature down to low and cover with a lid.

2 Allow the rice to simmer gently for about 8 minutes until the water has all been absorbed. DO NOT STIR! Tilt the saucepan to check that the liquid is all gone, then remove from the heat and place a clean tea towel over the top and place the lid back on. Allow to steam dry for 5–10 minutes – then, and only then, you can fluff it up using a fork for the perfect rice.

NOTE: For brown rice the measurements are 1 cup of rice to 1¾ cups of water, allow an extra 8–10 minutes for the water to be absorbed but otherwise the instructions are the same.

1. BASMATI RICE WITH CINNAMON, CARDAMOM AND FLAKED ALMONDS

INGREDIENTS   FEEDS 2

1 cup basmati rice

1 cinnamon stick

5 cardamom pods

1 tablespoon onion seeds

A small handful of flaked almonds

METHOD

1 Cook the rice as described above, but add the cinnamon stick and bruised cardamom pods at the start so the flavours infuse during cooking.

2 Once the rice has steamed add the onion seeds and flaked almonds and fluff up the rice using a fork. Remove the cardamom pods and cinnamon stick before serving.

2. BROWN RICE WITH GARLIC, NUTMEG AND CINNAMON

INGREDIENTS   FEEDS 2

1 cup brown rice
4 cloves of garlic
A knob of butter and splash of olive oil
Half a nutmeg, grated
1 teaspoon ground cinnamon

METHOD

1 Cook the rice as described, remembering that brown rice takes longer and absorbs more water.

2 Peel and finely slice the garlic cloves. Add the butter and oil to a large frying pan on a medium heat and when hot add the garlic, fry it for 2–3 minutes and add the nutmeg and cinnamon, cooking for a further minute. Add in the cooked rice and stir or toss until it is all coated with the wonderful flavours and heated through.

3. BROWN RICE WITH CUMIN, CORIANDER AND TURMERIC

INGREDIENTS   FEEDS 2

1 cup brown rice
1 teaspoon cumin seeds
1 teaspoon coriander seeds
1 teaspoon turmeric

METHOD

1 Cook the rice as described, remembering that brown rice takes longer and absorbs more water.

2 In a mortar and pestle bash up the cumin and coriander until finely ground. Toast them on a dry pan with the turmeric on a medium/high heat for 2–3 minutes until fragrant. Add the rice and give a good stir or toss until the rice and spices are well combined and heated through.

ROAST BUTTERNUT SQUASH
WITH CHILLI, ROSEMARY AND GARLIC

Butternut squash was something I had never tasted until I grew my own. It's a very versatile vegetable and it stores really well. This dish goes well with chicken, pork or fish and is a great substitute for potatoes.

FEEDS 4

INGREDIENTS

1 large or 2 small butternut squash (1kg)
6–8 cloves of garlic
1 red chilli
Few sprigs of rosemary
Olive oil
Sea salt and black pepper to season
½ lemon

METHOD

1 Preheat the oven to 190ºC.

2 Slice the squash in half lengthways, then in half again. Cut out the seeds section with a knife or scoop out with a spoon.

3 Peel the skin, as it can be a little tough, and cut the squash into wedges or chunks and place it in a roasting tray.

4 Put the cloves of garlic onto a chopping board and bash with the flat of a knife. Add them to the tray along with the finely chopped chilli and the rosemary. Drizzle over some oil, season with some salt and black pepper and toss it all together.

5 Roast in the preheated oven for about 45 minutes. When finished roasting squeeze the juice of a half a lemon over the top and serve.

ROAST CARROTS
WITH ORANGE AND CUMIN

This is one of my favourite dishes and comes fresh from my garden. I use young summer carrots. If they are from your own garden, don't peel them, just give them a good scrub. Any slightly thicker ones just slice down the centre. You can use any kind of carrot, but try and cut them to roughly the same size so they will cook at the same time. These work well with any roast dinner.

FEEDS 4

INGREDIENTS

Olive oil
A knob of butter
600g carrots
2 teaspoons cumin seeds
Sea salt and black pepper to season
1 orange

METHOD

1 Pour some oil and drop a knob of butter into an oven dish and place into an oven preheated to 190°C.

2 Prepare the carrots by cutting them to roughly the same size.

3 Remove the tray, ensuring that the butter has melted, and put in the carrots, sprinkle over the cumin seeds and season well. Cover with foil and place in the oven for around 30 minutes.

4 Take out of the oven and remove the foil. Add in the grated zest of the orange and a good squeeze of juice. Stir all around and place back into oven for 20 minutes.

5 Remove and serve right away.

ROASTED RED ONIONS WITH PORT AND BAY LEAVES

This is a wonderful-tasting side dish that works well with any meat dish. It is at its best with red onions straight from the ground.

FEEDS 4–6

INGREDIENTS

750g small red onions
Olive oil
10–12 bay leaves
Sea salt and black pepper to season
200ml port

METHOD

1 Preheat the oven to 180°C.

2 Trim the tops of the onions and peel, keeping the root end intact. Slice the onions from root to tip into eight wedges; the root end should hold the pieces together.

3 Pour some oil into a roasting tray and throw the onions into it. Give the bay leaves a twist to tear them but not the whole way through. Scatter them over, pushing them in through the onions. Season well and pour the port over it all.

4 Cover with foil and bung into the oven for 40 minutes. Take out of the oven and give a stir around. Place back in the oven without the foil for a further 30 minutes.

5 When ready the liquid should have reduced to a thick syrup. Serve hot, warm or cold.

ROASTED VEGETABLE MIX WITH MAPLE SYRUP

I'm a huge fan of roasted veg. It only takes a little bit of time to prepare and minimal looking after. This selection is my usual handy roast dinner accompaniment, but there is no end to the selections you can have.

INGREDIENTS

3 carrots
3 parsnips
2 courgettes
2 red onions
1 red pepper
1 yellow pepper
1 green pepper
5 cloves of garlic
Olive oil
Sea salt and black pepper to season
2 tablespoons maple syrup

FEEDS 4

METHOD

1 Preheat the oven to 200ºC.

2 Peel the carrots and parsnips and cut into batons. Wash the courgettes and cut into batons also. Peel the onions and cut into wedges. De-seed and slice the peppers. Bash the cloves of garlic with the flat of a knife.

3 Pour all the prepared vegetables into a roasting tray. Drizzle with oil and give a generous amount of seasoning. Place in oven for 30 minutes.

4 Remove from the oven and drizzle the maple syrup over the vegetable mix and give it a good toss around. Then pop it back into the oven for 10 minutes.

5 Serve hot and remove the garlic cloves if desired.

TIP: If you are feeling adventurous, then feel free to add flavouring to this dish – some herbs like rosemary, thyme, sage … spices like fennel, cumin or caraway seeds … wholegrain mustard, balsamic vinegar, soy sauce … basically whatever you like!

STUFFED SQUASH THREE WAYS

This is a great accompaniment to a meat dish, but I mainly have it as a lunch or flavour-packed night-time snack. There is no end to the variations you can have, it's all about the combination of flavours used in the filling. Here are a few of my favourite ones. In my opinion there is no right or wrong way with flavours, it's just about what works for you!

1. BUTTERNUT SQUASH WITH GARLIC AND GOAT'S CHEESE

FEEDS 2

INGREDIENTS

1 large butternut squash
Olive oil
1 clove of garlic

2 teaspoons chopped thyme
Half a red pepper
200g goat's cheese
1 tablespoon honey

METHOD

1 Preheat the oven to 190°C.

2 To prepare the squash slice it down the middle lengthways. Spoon out the seeds and soft fibres, then brush with olive oil.

3 Finely chop the garlic and thyme and finely slice the pepper. Pop these into the cavity in the 2 halves and place into the preheated oven.

4 Bake for 45–50 minutes. Remove from the oven and scoop out the filling along with about half of the flesh, mash it all together along with the goat's cheese and season well. Spoon it back into the cavities, spoon the honey over the top and bung back into the oven for a further 15 minutes.

2. BUTTERNUT SQUASH WITH BACON, CHEDDAR AND PEANUT BUTTER

FEEDS 2

INGREDIENTS

1 large butternut squash
Olive oil
2 tablespoons peanut butter
50g red cheddar, grated

3–4 rashers of streaky bacon, chopped
1 tablespoon chopped chives
Sea salt and black pepper to season

METHOD

1 Preheat the oven to 190ºC.

2 Prepare the squash as for recipe 1.

3 Put the peanut butter into the cavities along with half the cheese and bung into the oven for 45–50 minutes. In the meantime fry the chopped bacon for 2 minutes until coloured and crisp.

4 Mix the bacon and chives in with the soft squash when it comes out of the oven, season and top with the rest of the cheese. Pop the tray back into the oven for 15 minutes.

3. BUTTERNUT SQUASH WITH YELLOW PEPPER AND BALSAMIC VINEGAR

INGREDIENTS

1 large butternut squash
Olive oil
2 medium onions
1 clove of garlic, peeled
Half a yellow pepper
1 tablespoon balsamic vinegar
Sea salt and black pepper to season

FEEDS
2

METHOD

1 Preheat the oven to 190ºC.

2 Prepare the squash as for recipe 1.

3 This time put the squash into the oven just brushed with oil. Sweat the sliced onion and chopped garlic in a pan. Add the yellow pepper, de-seeded and finely chopped. Turn the heat up full, then add the balsamic vinegar and stir until the vinegar has all but disappeared.

4 When the squash has been in for 45–50 minutes, take it out and mix the onion mixture with the soft squash flesh, season well and bung back into the oven for 15 minutes.

SWEET POTATO WEDGES

Simple, warming, healthy and flavoursome ... Bingo! Sweet potatoes are a 'superfood', packed with antioxidants that boost the immune system to fight against viral infections and even cancer. They are energy boosting too, as well as tasting fantastic!

FEEDS 2

INGREDIENTS

4 medium sweet potatoes
Olive oil
Cayenne pepper
Sea salt and black pepper to season

METHOD

1 Lightly scrub the sweet potatoes and cut them into chunky full-length wedges.

2 Preheat the oven to 200°C.

3 Parboil the wedges for 3–4 minutes in a large saucepan of salted water, then drain in a colander and allow them to steam dry for a few minutes.

4 Place on a lightly oiled tray and drizzle with a little oil, then sprinkle with cayenne pepper, sea salt and black pepper.

5 Roast in the oven for 20 minutes.

6 Can be served with a dip of your choice, e.g. sweet chilli sauce, sour cream and chive.

YORKSHIRE PUDDINGS

Want to hear something good? Yorkshire puddings are so easy to make it's ridiculous! They make a great addition to any Sunday roast (especially beef). Give these a try and you won't look back!

MAKES 10–12

INGREDIENTS

1 mug of milk
Just under 1 mug of self-raising flour
1 egg
Pinch of salt
Olive oil

METHOD

1 While the oven is on for your roast, put in a muffin tray to heat about 5 minutes before the roast is due to come out to rest.

2 Put the milk, flour and egg in a liquidiser with a pinch of salt and whiz until smooth, or alternatively you can whisk by hand until smooth (use a bit of elbow grease!).

3 Remove the hot muffin tray from the oven and pour a little oil into each compartment. Pour the batter into each compartment up to half full.

4 Remove your roast and place the full tray into the oven for 20 minutes at 220°C but DO NOT open the door until they are cooked, risen and golden or they won't rise as well as they should.

DESSERTS AND TREATS

AFTER EIGHT CHEESECAKE

FEEDS / 6–8

INGREDIENTS

15 digestive biscuits
50g butter
300g box of After Eight dinner mints
   (2 boxes if decorating like the photo)
300g low-fat cream cheese
90g granulated sugar
1 pint of double cream

This cheesecake is very light and the mint helps a full belly after a hearty main course. It is very quick and easy to make and can be made a day in advance to take a bit of pressure off if you have guests coming. Just cover with cling film and it will quite happily sit in your fridge overnight.

METHOD

1 Put the digestive biscuits into a large, strong sandwich bag and bash with a rolling pin, or put through a blender to crush them.

2 Put the crushed biscuits in a bowl, melt the butter over a medium heat, pour it over the crushed biscuits and mix thoroughly.

3 Put the mix into a 23cm/9in spring-form tin and firm down to form a compact even layer (I use a potato masher for this). Place in the fridge for half an hour.

4 Roughly chop up the contents of one box of After Eights and set aside.

5 Place the cream cheese and sugar into a bowl, stir to loosen the cheese, then pour in the double cream. Whisk this mix until it starts to firm. Add in the chopped dinner mints and whisk the whole mixture again.

6 To decorate the cake as I did for the picture, place the contents of the second box of mints around the inside of the cake tin BEFORE POURING THE FILLING IN, so that when you remove the sides of the tin you are left with a 'wall' of dinner mints that are held in place by the cream.

7 Pour the filling over the top of the biscuit base and smooth out with a spatula. Allow to set in the fridge for at least 2 hours.

APPLE TART

Apple tarts are very nostalgic things ... memories of my mother baking, my father going to collect apples and of course asking for slice after slice at Halloween, trying to find the hidden 20p coin wrapped in tinfoil in it — an old tradition ... maybe 50p if you were lucky.

INGREDIENTS

3 cooking apples

3 cloves

5 tablespoons granulated sugar

300g flaky pastry (see p. 278)

1 beaten egg

MAKES 1 DINNER PLATE-SIZED TART

METHOD

1 Peel and core the apples and slice them thinly.

2 Place a medium saucepan on a medium/high heat and add a small splash of water. Add the apple slices, cloves and sugar. Stew the apples for about 15 minutes, stirring occasionally. When cooked pick out the three cloves. Allow the stewed apples to cool fully.

3 Preheat the oven to 180°C. Roll out half the pastry thinly and lay it over a deep dinner plate; push it right down making sure it is tight to the plate all over. Carefully trim around the edge with a sharp knife.

4 Place the stewed apples into the middle of the pastry and spread evenly with a spoon, to about 3cm/1½in from the edge. Wet the rim with cold water using a pastry brush or your finger.

5 Roll out the remaining pastry a little thicker and lay it carefully over the top. Gently firm down, getting rid of air bubbles. Using your fingers or a fork, firmly press around the rim sealing the two pieces of pastry together and again trim around the edge with a sharp knife. Gently stab the top of the tart a few times with a knife.

6 Glaze the tart with the beaten egg using a pastry brush and place in the preheated oven for 25 minutes or until golden brown on top. Serve hot with ice-cream or freshly whipped cream.

AWA'S KEY LIME PIE

FEEDS 8

INGREDIENTS

15 digestive biscuits
150g butter
Juice and zest of 3–4 limes
1 pint of double cream
A large can of condensed milk

Key lime pie is a lot like cheesecake to make – no real time or effort goes into it, but it is worth making. It is very refreshing and has a beautiful sharpness to it. My sister Andrea (Awa) made this for me on a visit back up home and I fell in love with it straightaway. It can be made in a spring-form tin or in individual portions using pastry rings.

METHOD

1 Place the biscuits into a sandwich bag, seal it and bash the hell out of it with a rolling pin to break up the biscuits. Melt the butter in a medium saucepan and pour in the mashed biscuits, stir well and empty the contents into a 23cm/9in spring-form tin. Firm down evenly (I find a potato masher works well here) and place in the fridge for 20–30 minutes.

2 Roll the limes on the countertop firmly with the palm of your hand to loosen up the juice. Zest them with a zester or a small grater – only the green outer skin though – then halve them and juice them.

3 In a large mixing bowl combine the lime juice, double cream and condensed milk. Whisk together with an electric mixer until it starts to thicken, then add in the lime zest. Whisk again until quite thick.

4 Scoop this mix out on top of the biscuit base, smooth over and return to the fridge for at least 2 hours to set.

CARROT CAKE

Carrot cake combines wonderful strong flavours that gel together so well. You can play around with different ingredients, but this is probably as 'classic' as it gets.

INGREDIENTS FEEDS 8

215g plain flour
200g caster sugar
1½ teaspoons bicarbonate of soda
1 teaspoon baking powder
1 teaspoon cinnamon
½ teaspoon nutmeg
½ teaspoon ground cloves
½ teaspoon allspice
A pinch of salt
150ml sunflower oil

3 medium eggs
2 large/3 medium carrots
A handful of walnuts
A handful of sultanas

For the cream cheese frosting:
225g cream cheese
75g unsalted butter
2 teaspoons vanilla extract
450g icing sugar
Zest of 1 orange

METHOD

1 Preheat the oven to 180°C.

2 Grease a 1lb/450g loaf tin evenly and line the bottom with parchment paper.

3 In a large mixing bowl combine the flour, sugar, bicarbonate of soda, baking powder, spices and salt. In a smaller bowl whisk together the oil and eggs.

4 Grate the carrots and chop the walnuts.

5 Pour the egg and oil mixture into the dry ingredients and mix thoroughly with a wooden spoon. Add the carrots, walnuts and sultanas to the mix, stir until combined and pour the mix into the loaf tin, then pop in the oven for 40 minutes.

6 After 40 minutes stick a skewer in the cake – it will come out clean if the cake is fully cooked. If not give it another 5 minutes and try again. Cool in the tin for 10 minutes, then transfer to a cooling rack.

7 To make the frosting, beat the cheese, butter and vanilla extract together with an electric whisk, then gradually beat in the icing sugar. Fold in the orange zest using a spatula. When the carrot cake has fully cooled, spread the frosting generously over the top.

CHOCOLATE CHIP BROWNIES

INGREDIENTS

150g plain chocolate
225g softened butter
100g white chocolate
75g pistachio nuts
225g self-raising flour
125g caster sugar
4 medium eggs
Icing sugar (for dusting)

MAKES 12

Not much can be said about these legends except ...
enjoy chocolatey goodness responsibly!

METHOD

1 Preheat the oven to 180°C.

2 Line a 33cm/13in x 23cm/9in baking tray with baking paper.

3 Break up the plain chocolate into pieces and place in a heatproof bowl along with the softened butter. Place the bowl over a saucepan of simmering water. Stir until melted, then leave to cool slightly.

4 Chop the white chocolate and pistachio nuts.

5 Sift the flour into another bowl and add the caster sugar, then set aside.

6 Beat the eggs and stir into the melted chocolate, then pour the mixture into the flour and sugar and beat together well.

7 Stir in the chopped nuts and white chocolate, then pour into the baking tray. Even out the mixture with a spatula. Bake in the oven for 30–35 minutes until risen and once pressed with your finger it springs back.

8 When cooked, leave to cool in the tin for 15 minutes, then turn out onto a cooling rack and dust with icing sugar. Allow to cool fully before cutting into twelve pieces.

EASY BANOFFEE PIE

FEEDS 8–10

This is so easy and quick to make, it's definitely one to get the kids involved with, especially since the caramel is coming straight from a tin. I add some food colouring to my whipped double cream just to add a bit of colour and flare to it. Tradition is to have a biscuit base with a Banoffee but I go for a sweet short-crust pastry base. If you can make up the pastry case in advance then you will have this made in minutes. You can buy caramel in a tin in any supermarket these days, so it makes this dessert very simple.

INGREDIENTS

23cm/9in pre-made sweet pastry case

1 tin of pre-made caramel

4 ripe bananas

300ml double cream

1 teaspoon vanilla essence

1 teaspoon food colouring (optional)

1 bar of dark chocolate to serve

METHOD

1 Spread the caramel on the pastry case in an even layer using a palate knife.

2 Peel and slice the bananas at an angle and lay them on the caramel in an even layer, then set this aside.

3 Whip the double cream with the vanilla essence until fairly thick. If using the food colouring, just gently fold it into the cream to create a ripple effect.

4 Spread the cream on top of the pie, using a spatula or put into a piping bag and pipe on top.

5 To finish, turn the bar of chocolate upside down so the smooth side is pointing up, let it rest on the worktop and against the front of your hip – and with a knife, shave off thin curls pulling the knife towards you firmly on the chocolate. Please be very careful while doing this, as you could injure yourself if the knife slips. Sprinkle these over the top of the pie and keep it refrigerated until ready to serve.

ETON MESS

There are all kinds of different takes on this dessert and many ways to tweak it. Feel free to play around with it. Some desserts take very little effort to make but still taste heavenly — this is one of them.

INGREDIENTS

225g fresh strawberries
2 tablespoons caster sugar
Half a lemon
284ml carton of double cream
6 mini meringue nests

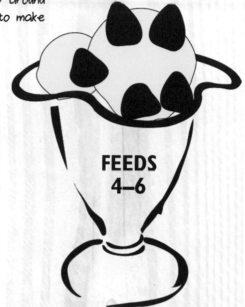

FEEDS 4–6

METHOD

1 Wash the strawberries and pick out the stalk. Chop half of them and place them in a small saucepan on a medium heat, sprinkle with 1 tablespoon of sugar and a squeeze of lemon juice. Stew them for a few minutes, then pour them into a bowl to cool.

2 Cut the other strawberries into slices or quarters.

3 Whip up the double cream in a mixing bowl with the second spoonful of caster sugar. Lightly crush the meringue nests.

4 Mix the stewed strawberries and crushed meringues into the cream and divide out into dessert glasses, top with the cut strawberries and serve.

GUILT FREE
PANNA COTTA

Panna cotta is normally made using double cream. The double cream does give it a deep richness; however, when made my way it is lighter but still as tasty, minus the double cream's double calories.

INGREDIENTS

600ml semi-skimmed milk

1 vanilla pod or dash of vanilla extract

125g caster sugar

4 sheets of leaf gelatine

200ml low-fat natural yogurt

For the sauce

200g frozen blueberries

2 tablespoons caster sugar

2 tablespoons lemon juice

FEEDS 4

METHOD

1 Pour the milk into a medium-sized saucepan, split the vanilla pod down the middle and scrape the seeds into the milk, or add the vanilla extract. Heat the milk gently and add the sugar, stirring until it dissolves. In the meantime place the gelatine leaves into some cold water for a few minutes to soften them.

2 Once the milk starts to bubble, remove it from the heat. Squeeze out the excess water from the gelatine leaves, add them to the milk and stir until they dissolve. Allow the mixture to cool before passing through a fine sieve into a mixing bowl.

3 Once the mixture has cooled completely add the yogurt and stir to mix. Pour the mixture into small pudding moulds and chill them in the fridge for at least 2 hours or ideally overnight.

4 To make the sauce, thaw the blueberries and add them along with the sugar and lemon juice to a small saucepan. Bring to a simmer and cook for a few minutes until the berries are heated through. Transfer to a bowl and allow to cool slightly.

5 To unmould the panna cottas, dip each mould into a bowl of warm water for a few seconds, then carefully turn over onto a serving plate, give a little shake and they should slide out.

6 Serve with the dressing of blueberries in their sauce.

LAVENDER SHORTCAKES WITH STRAWBERRIES

INGREDIENTS

MAKES 10–12

A few sprigs of fresh or dried lavender
100g softened butter
50g caster sugar
1 egg yolk
150g plain flour
350g strawberries
1 tablespoon orange juice

These shortcakes are very easily made and are lovely by themselves, just with a cup of tea. You could try chopped rosemary instead of the lavender for a change.

METHOD

1 Preheat the oven to 190°C and lightly grease two baking trays. Rub or pick the flowers off the lavender sprigs.

2 Beat the butter and sugar together with an electric mixer until light and fluffy, add in the egg yolk and the lavender flowers. Then add the flour and mix to a soft dough with a wooden spoon.

3 Roll out the dough on a lightly floured work surface to about 3mm thick (it does tend to break up easily but work patiently with it). Cut out 10–12 biscuits with an 8cm/3in cookie cutter.

4 Transfer gently to the baking sheets and bake in oven for 10 minutes until golden.

5 Allow to cool for a minute before transferring to a cooling rack.

6 Wash and hull the strawberries. Slice two-thirds of them and place in a mixing bowl. Purée the remaining strawberries with the orange juice and push through a sieve to remove the seeds. Stir the purée into the strawberry slices and serve with the shortcakes and perhaps a dollop of fresh whipped cream.

LEMON MERINGUE PIE

A home-made lemon meringue pie can seem daunting to some people. All I can say is follow this set of instructions and it won't go wrong.

INGREDIENTS

280g granulated sugar
30g cornflour
A pinch of salt
3 lemons zested and juiced –
   you will need 125ml of juice
1 large egg, plus one egg yolk
1 teaspoon butter

23cm/9in pastry case
   (shop-bought or make your own – see p. 283)

For the meringue
3 large egg whites
A pinch of salt
A dash of vanilla extract
115g caster sugar

**FEEDS
6–8**

METHOD

1 In a large saucepan, mix together the sugar, cornflour and salt. Gradually whisk in 250ml boiling water to make a smooth sauce. Place the saucepan on a medium heat and continue whisking while bringing to the boil, then reduce the heat slightly and cook for a further 2 minutes without whisking. Remove from the heat.

2 In a small mixing bowl whisk the lemon juice, zest, egg and egg yolk together. Carefully whisk a little of the cooked hot sauce into the lemon/egg mix, then whisk this all back into the cooked hot sauce in the saucepan.

3 Return the saucepan to a medium heat and, while stirring, bring to a simmer. Add the butter and continue stirring until it thickens (this can take a while but stick with it). Once thickened, remove from the heat and pour into the pastry case and allow to cool so it starts to set.

4 In the meantime, preheat the oven to 170°C and get to making the meringue. Put the egg whites in a large, clean mixing bowl. Whisk them until light and frothy, then add the salt and vanilla extract. Whisk this well until it forms soft peaks. Add the caster sugar a tablespoon at a time, while continually whisking until all the sugar is used and the meringue forms stiff peaks. Using a spatula put the meringue on top of the pie and using a pallet knife gently spread it evenly. Pat the meringue with the pallet knife all over to form peaks.

5 Place the pie into the oven and bake for about 15 minutes until the peaks have coloured. Remove from the oven and allow to cool fully before serving – this normally takes about 2 hours.

LIME MOUSSE

INGREDIENTS

1 sheet leaf gelatine
2 limes
85g caster sugar
1 large egg white
100ml crème fraiche

MAKES 4 SMALL MOUSSES

These little mousses are simple to make up and can be made well in advance so it takes the pressure off when it comes to cooking dinner. They are really light, sweet and have a nice refreshing sharpness from the lime.

METHOD

1 Soak the gelatine leaf in cold water for a few minutes to soften. Zest one of the limes and set the zest aside.

2 Squeeze the two limes and put the juice in a measuring jug and top up to 100ml with cold water. Pour this into a small saucepan and add half the sugar, stir over a low heat to dissolve the sugar, then bring to a simmer and remove from the heat.

3 Squeeze out the gelatine leaf and add to the lime syrup, stir until it dissolves and allow the mixture to cool completely.

4 Beat the egg white in a small mixing bowl until it forms stiff peaks, then beat in the rest of the sugar, a spoonful at a time.

5 In a separate bowl lightly beat the crème fraiche, then stir the lime syrup into it. It will be very loose but fold through the egg white mix and spoon into small serving glasses.

6 Chill the mousses in the fridge for at least 2 hours to firm up. Decorate with the lime zest.

RED VELVET CUPCAKES

Red velvet cupcakes are basically chocolate buns with food colouring! Growing up we always called them 'buns' or 'Queen cakes', but somewhere along the way we got Americanised and started calling them cupcakes.

INGREDIENTS

100g self-raising flour
15g cocoa powder
1 teaspoon baking powder
115g softened butter
115g caster sugar
2 medium eggs
2 teaspoons red food colouring

For the frosting
200g cream cheese
6 tablespoons icing sugar
200ml double cream

MAKES 12

METHOD

1 Preheat the oven to 180°C.

2 Line a muffin tray with 12 muffin cases.

3 Sift the flour, cocoa powder and baking powder into a large mixing bowl. Add the softened butter, caster sugar, eggs and the food colouring (be very careful with this as it stains anything it touches!). Mix all together with a wooden spoon or with an electric hand-held mixer on a slow setting.

4 When the mixture is well combined, spoon or pipe it into the muffin cases, to just over halfway up.

5 Bake in the preheated oven for 15 minutes – they are ready if they spring back when you press them gently. Cool on a wire rack.

6 For the frosting, gently whisk together the cream cheese and icing sugar in a bowl, then add the double cream. Whisk again until slightly stiffened.

7 Pipe the frosting on top of the cupcakes in whatever designs you like ... get the kids involved! Everyone will love red velvet cupcakes!

RED WINE POACHED PEARS

These are a little time consuming but very much worth the effort. Not only do they look elegant, but they taste superb served with ice-cream with chopped hazelnuts sprinkled over it.

FEEDS 4

INGREDIENTS

400ml red wine
150g granulated sugar
2 tablespoons lemon juice
2 teaspoons vanilla extract
1 cinnamon stick
1 star anise
4 pears

METHOD

1   Combine all the ingredients except for the pears into a saucepan that will fit four pears and place on a hot hob. Stir over the heat until the sugar dissolves, then bring to the boil and reduce to a steady simmer.

2   In the meantime core the pears from the bottom, scooping out the core and seeds without disturbing the top and stem. Then peel the pears carefully.

3   Add the pears to the simmering wine syrup and allow them to simmer untouched for 12–14 minutes, then turn them over and simmer for a further 8–10 minutes until tender when pierced with a fork. Carefully remove them from the saucepan and allow to cool.

4   Turn up the heat and reduce the wine syrup by half. Pour this over the pears when serving.

RHUBARB AND GINGER TARTLETS

Rhubarb and ginger are both good for the stomach and digestive system.

One could say the perfect dessert! Shortcrust cases are readily available in the supermarkets, so you can cut down on work.

INGREDIENTS

A small knob of butter

3 stems of rhubarb – chopped into 2½cm/1in pieces

6–8 tablespoons caster sugar

1 orange, juiced

1 tablespoon honey

A thumb-sized piece of ginger, peeled

1 teaspoon good vanilla extract

150ml low-fat natural yogurt

4 small shortcrust pastry cases – shop-bought or home-made

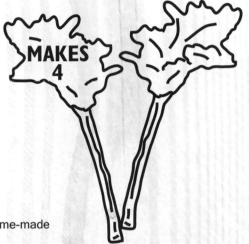

MAKES
4

METHOD

1 Melt the butter over a medium heat. Add the rhubarb, caster sugar, juice of the orange and the honey, and stir until the sugar dissolves.

2 Grate in the ginger and stir well. Allow the mixture to simmer while the rhubarb softens, but do not allow the fruit to break down completely. Taste for sweetness and add a little more sugar if needed. Allow to cool slightly.

3 While the mix is cooling, add the vanilla extract to the natural yogurt and whisk through.

4 Spoon the rhubarb into the pastry cases and serve with the vanilla yogurt.

RICE PUDDING

This is a recipe straight from home. My mother made rice pudding all the time: comforting goodness in a bowl. I normally don't do measuring by cup measures; however, I do with this recipe, as it's simpler as long as the ratios are correct. And by cup I mean any size cup, mug, whatever you like as long as you use the same one for all the measurements.

INGREDIENTS

¾ cup pudding rice
2 cups milk
⅓ cup granulated sugar
A pinch of salt
1 egg, beaten
⅔ cup raisins
A knob of butter
½ teaspoon of vanilla extract
Cinnamon to serve (optional)

FEEDS 4

METHOD

1 In a medium saucepan bring 1½ cups of water to the boil. Stir in the rice and turn down to a low heat. Simmer for about 20 minutes until all the water has been absorbed.

2 In a large saucepan combine the rice (you should have 1½ cups of cooked rice) with 1½ cups of milk (keeping half a cup of milk aside).

3 Add the sugar and salt and bring to a low simmer for about 20 minutes until thick and creamy. At that point add in the remaining milk, beaten egg and raisins and cook for a further 2 minutes stirring constantly.

4 Remove from the heat and stir in the butter and vanilla extract.

5 Serve hot or cold with a sprinkle of cinnamon.

SUMMER BERRY, WHITE CHOCOLATE AND RUM CRUMBLE

INGREDIENTS

300g strawberries
150g raspberries
150g blueberries
150g white chocolate
A sprinkle of white rum (optional and the amount is flexible!)

For the crumble

150g plain flour
75g butter
75g soft brown sugar
½ teaspoon cinnamon
50g chopped almonds

FEEDS 4

This is a beautiful simple dessert with fresh flavours that will leave you longing for more. Even without the crumble topping this is delicious cooked in the oven for about 8 minutes and served with ice-cream.

METHOD

1 Wash the fruit, hull and halve the strawberries.

2 Preheat oven to 180°C.

3 Pour the prepared fruit into a suitable-sized oven dish or if you prefer individual crumbles, four smaller oven dishes. Roughly chop the white chocolate and sprinkle over the fruit. Add the splash of rum (if using).

4 For the crumble, place the flour into a mixing bowl, cube the butter and rub it in with your fingers until it resembles fine breadcrumbs. Stir in the sugar, cinnamon and almonds until well combined.

5 Sprinkle over the topping and bake in the oven for about 20 minutes or until the crumble is golden brown and the fruit is bubbling around the edges.

6 Serve with fresh whipped cream or ice-cream.

VICTORIA SPONGE CAKE

I make this classic sponge on a very regular basis for customers looking for custom-made celebration cakes. I normally cover mine in fondant icing in all sorts of shapes and designs. However, this is how a Victoria Sponge is traditionally presented — with some freshly whipped cream, jam and fresh strawberries.

INGREDIENTS MAKES ONE DEEP CAKE (½ THE MIX FOR A SHALLOW CAKE)

350g caster sugar

350g unsalted butter, softened

6 medium eggs

350g self-raising flour

A pinch of salt

284ml carton of fresh cream

1 teaspoon vanilla extract (optional)

1 punnet of fresh strawberries

Strawberry jam

Icing sugar to dust

METHOD

1 Preheat the oven to 160°C.

2 Place the caster sugar and softened butter in a large mixing bowl and beat together with an electric hand-held mixer until pale in colour.

3 Add the eggs two at a time, while still beating, mixing well between each two. (I break them all into a jug first so they're easy to pour in.)

4 Next sift the flour and salt into the same bowl and using a spatula slowly fold this into the wet mix until it is well mixed.

5 Line a 23cm/9in cake tin with baking paper (or if it's a spring-form tin in good nick, grease it well with the paper from the butter) and pour the mixture in. Even it out with a spatula and place the tin on the middle shelf of the oven. Bake for 1 hour 15 minutes. Do not be tempted to open the oven door for at least the first hour as this can cause the cake to sink. When it's ready the centre should spring back up when gently pressed; you can also check using a skewer. (If using half the quantity then it should be ready in 40 minutes.)

6 Remove the cake carefully from the tin and allow it to cool on a wire rack.

7 In the meantime whip the fresh cream in a clean mixing bowl and whip in the vanilla extract (if using). Hull and slice the strawberries into thick slices.

8 When the cake is cool, carefully cut it horizontally with a large sharp knife or a cake saw. Spread a generous layer of jam on each half, then add the cream and a layer of strawberries to one half and top with the other half, jam side down. You can also cut the cake in three: spread a generous layer of jam on the bottom, then half the cream, place the middle layer of cake on top, then the other half of the cream, then a layer of strawberries, then the top of the cake.

9 Sift a little icing sugar on top before serving.

HOME-MADE ALTERNATIVES

APPLE SAUCE

Apple sauce to accompany pork.

INGREDIENTS

**MAKES
1 JAR**

3 cooking apples

3 cloves

5 tablespoons granulated sugar

METHOD

1 Peel and core the apples and slice thinly.

2 Place a medium saucepan on a medium/high heat and add a small splash of water. Add the apple slices, cloves and sugar. Stew the apples for about 15 minutes, stirring occasionally.

3 When cooled, remove the cloves and transfer into a sterilised jar and keep in the fridge.

COLESLAW

This coleslaw is quick to make and comes in very handy, especially during BBQ season.

INGREDIENTS

FEEDS 6

½ white cabbage

2 carrots

½ onion

6 tablespoons low-fat natural yogurt

2 tablespoons low-fat mayonnaise

½ teaspoon Dijon mustard

METHOD

1 Using a box grater or the grater attachment of a food processor, grate the cabbage, carrots and onion.

2 In a large mixing bowl stir together the yogurt, mayonnaise and Dijon mustard, then add in the grated vegetables and combine thoroughly.

3 This mix will keep in the fridge for three days.

BASIC BANANA BREAD

I have called this 'Basic Banana Bread' because there are lots of things you can add into the recipe like nuts, seeds, dried fruit, etc., but this is plain. However, the taste is far from 'basic' or 'plain'. Banana bread, whilst in the oven, fills the kitchen with a warming sweet smell. A slice fresh out of the oven with a cup of tea ... well, I'll let you decide!

INGREDIENTS

MAKES 1 LOAF

285g plain flour
1 teaspoon bicarbonate of soda
½ teaspoon salt
225g caster sugar
110g unsalted butter, plus extra for greasing
2 eggs
4 ripe bananas, mashed
85ml buttermilk
1 teaspoon vanilla extract

METHOD

1 Preheat the oven to 180ºC.

2 Grease a 450g/1lb loaf tin with some butter.

3 Sift the flour, bicarbonate of soda and salt into a medium bowl.

4 In a large mixing bowl cream together the sugar and butter using an electric mixer until light and fluffy-looking. Add the eggs, mashed bananas, buttermilk and vanilla extract and mix well.

5 Fold the flour mix into the wet ingredients with a wooden spoon until just incorporated (no need to mix too thoroughly) and pour the mix into the greased tin.

6 Place in the middle shelf of the oven and bake for 1 hour until golden brown and cooked through.

7 Remove from the oven and allow to cool for a few minutes in the tin before turning out onto a cooling rack.

TIP: If you have no buttermilk for the recipe, use ordinary milk with a teaspoon and a half of lemon juice or vinegar whisked in to curdle it ... it works a treat!

CIABATTA

This recipe is time-consuming, but great if you are about the house and not too worried about sitting waiting for it. It is really worth the effort. Make the sponge the day before. Strong white flour or bread flour has a slightly higher percentage of gluten (roughly 2%) and this gives the bread its more elastic, chewy texture.

INGREDIENTS MAKES 2 MEDIUM LOAVES

Sponge

2 tablespoons warm water

⅛ teaspoon fast action yeast

100ml room temperature water

115g strong white flour

Bread

2 tablespoons warm milk

½ teaspoon fast action yeast

125ml room temperature water

1 tablespoon olive oil

230g strong white flour

1½ teaspoons salt

METHOD

To make the sponge

1 Stir the warm water and yeast together and allow to stand for 5 minutes until creamy. Transfer to a clean bowl and add the water and flour, then stir for 5 minutes constantly. Cover with cling film and keep at room temperature for 12–24 hours.

To make the bread

1 Stir together the milk and yeast and let stand for 5 minutes until creamy.

2 Using an electric mixer with a dough hook, combine the milk mixture, sponge mixture, water, oil and flour on a low speed until all the flour is mixed in.

3 Beat on medium for 3–4 minutes, then add the salt.

4 Beat for a further 4–5 minutes.

5 Scrape the wet dough out into a large, oiled bowl and cover with a damp tea towel. Allow to prove (rise) for 1½ hours at room temperature.

6 Turn the dough out onto a floured surface and cut into two pieces. This will be wet and sticky. Transfer each piece onto a baking sheet covered in baking paper. Form into irregular ovals, dust with flour and dimple using your finger. Cover again with a damp tea towel and allow to prove for a further 2 hours.

7 20 minutes before the end of proving time preheat the oven to 220°C.

8 Bake for 20 minutes until lightly golden. Cool on a wire rack once baked.

EASY DRESSINGS TO WOW

It's very easy to throw together a tasty dressing for a salad. I make mine up in sterilised jam jars for sheer handiness. Here are three of my favourites.

1. HONEY AND MUSTARD DRESSING

INGREDIENTS

3 tablespoons low-fat mayonnaise

3 tablespoons white wine vinegar

3 tablespoons olive oil

1 tablespoon honey

1 teaspoon Dijon mustard

Juice of half a lemon

Black pepper

METHOD

1   Place all ingredients into a clean jar, give a light whisk just to loosen them, then seal the lid and shake until combined.

2. STICKY RED WINE REDUCTION DRESSING

INGREDIENTS

Glass of red wine

50ml balsamic vinegar

Splash of soy sauce

Splash of oyster sauce

1 tablespoon honey

Black pepper

Glug of olive oil

METHOD

1 Pour the red wine into a small pan and bring to the boil, let it reduce by half, then add the balsamic vinegar, soy sauce, oyster sauce, honey and black pepper to taste. Give it all a good mix and cook for a further 2 minutes, then allow to cool slightly. Pour it into a clean jar with the oil and, with the lid on tight, give it a good shake.

3. ANCHOVY AND GARLIC DRESSING

INGREDIENTS

¼ clove of garlic, peeled
2 anchovies
1 tablespoon crème fraiche
A good pinch of grated Parmesan cheese
Juice of 1 lemon
Olive oil – about 3 times the volume of the lemon juice
Sea salt and black pepper to taste

METHOD

1 Mash the garlic and anchovies in a mortar and pestle, then scrape into a clean jar and whisk in the crème fraiche, grated Parmesan cheese, lemon juice and oil. Season to taste.

2 Give it all a good shake with the lid on tight.

EMERGENCY VEGETABLE STOCK

This is my 'Emergency vegetable stock'. By this I mean that you have a dinner in mind, you're just about to start cooking and realise you have no stock. This recipe will pull you out of a hole and in less than 15 minutes! Even better, this stock is fresh and won't have the additives and salt levels that bought stock cubes have.

INGREDIENTS

1 carrot
1 onion
2 stalks of celery
1 fat clove of garlic, peeled

1 bay leaf
Olive oil
5–6 whole peppercorns

MAKES 1 LITRE OF STOCK

METHOD

1 Grate the carrot, onion and celery. Mince the garlic and tear or finely shred the bay leaf.

2 Pour some oil into a medium saucepan and add all the ingredients and gently sweat for 3–4 minutes over a medium heat.

3 Pour a litre of water into the saucepan and turn the heat up full to bring to the boil and then reduce to a simmer for 5 minutes.

4 Strain through a sieve and *voilà* - you have an instant stock to add to your recipe!

50/50 HONEY AND SEEDED LOAF

This bread is one of the nicest I have made, and can be made from all strong white flour if you like. The beauty of home cooking is you can chop and change recipes to suit yourself ... they are not written in stone! This version consists of half white flour and half wholemeal flour. This is one of the first ever 'home-made' things I made and I'm glad I did!

INGREDIENTS

MAKES 1 LARGE LOAF OR 2 MEDIUM LOAVES

225g strong white flour

225g wholemeal flour

1½ teaspoons fine sea salt

7g sachet of dried baker's yeast

2 tablespoons mixed seeds

2 tablespoons dried fruit (optional)

3 tablespoons olive oil

2 tablespoons honey

275ml lukewarm water

A splash of milk to glaze

A teaspoon of sunflower seeds to sprinkle

METHOD

1 Pour the strong white flour, the wholemeal flour and salt into a large mixing bowl, add in the yeast and the seeds (and fruit if using) and give this all a good stir around.

2 Make a well in the centre and pour in the oil, honey and water and stir with a wooden spoon until well combined. The dough should be soft but not sticky.

3 Form the dough into a ball in the bowl, then turn out onto a lightly floured work surface and knead for 10 minutes until smooth.

4 Place the dough into a clean, oiled bowl, cover with a damp tea towel and let the dough rise in a warm spot in the kitchen until it has doubled in size. This normally takes about an hour.

5 When the dough has risen 'punch' the air out of it in the bowl, then move onto a lightly floured work surface and knead lightly for a minute. Divide the dough in half (if making two loaves) and shape however you please.

6 Place the dough onto an oiled baking sheet and cover again with the tea towel until it has almost doubled in size.

7 In the meantime preheat your oven to 200°C. When the dough has almost doubled in size brush a thin layer of milk over it, sprinkle with the sunflower seeds and bake for about 25 minutes until golden in colour. To know if your loaf is cooked through tap the underside – there should be a hollow sound.

8 Cool on a wire rack ... if you can resist temptation long enough, although not many can with home-made bread!

FLAVOURED OILS

Olive oil can be infused with all sorts of flavours and flavour combinations: chilli, garlic, herbs, spices etc. Here are three of my regulars.

Rosemary and garlic:
1 or 2 sprigs of rosemary and a fat clove of garlic, peeled

Basil and black pepper:
2 sprigs of basil and 8–10 black peppercorns

Chilli and garlic:
1–2 dried chillies and 1 fat clove of garlic, peeled

METHOD

1 Infuse the flavouring of your choice in 300ml of olive oil for a few days before using. The flavours will get stronger the longer you leave them in, so if you like after a week you can strain the oil out into a clean sterilized bottle. The flavoured oils will keep for 5–6 weeks.

They can be used in cooking or for drizzling.

GORGEOUS HOME-MADE FLAKY PASTRY

This is my mum's recipe. When I moved out of home and bought pies, tarts and the like, I would be eating them wondering what the hell went wrong! So I got the recipe, tweaked it a little bit and it now has a very strict set of instructions, but if you follow them carefully you will never buy pastry again! Yes, it's that good! The secret of this recipe is not to overdo the work.

INGREDIENTS

240g plain flour and extra for rolling
Pinch of salt
180g margarine at room temperature
Cold water to mix
30g lard at room temperature

MAKES ABOUT 500g OF PASTRY

METHOD

1 Put the flour in a mixing bowl, then add the salt. Cut 120g of the margarine in small pieces into the bowl. Now get in with clean hands and lightly rub the margarine through the flour.

2 Add the water gradually while mixing with a knife until it just about forms a dough. Empty the mixing bowl out onto a floured work surface, form the dough into a square and roll out into a rectangle: one roll of the rolling pin should suffice.

3 Cut the remaining margarine and the lard into small pieces and spread some of it onto the rolled-out pastry in small clumps. Roll up the pastry like a swiss roll, then turn the pastry ninety degrees and roll it out again. Repeat this process until all the margarine and lard has all been used.

Note how the pastry is kneaded and handled as little as possible.

4 Fold up the last time and wrap in cling film or foil and put in the fridge for at least an hour before using.

5 The pastry can be frozen at this point.

MINT SAUCE

This sauce is very simple to make and will accompany any lamb dish wonderfully.

INGREDIENTS

FEEDS 4–6

The leaves from a large bunch of mint
1 tablespoon caster sugar
4 tablespoons red wine vinegar
1 tablespoon olive oil

METHOD

1 Finely chop the mint leaves and add them to a mortar and pestle, give them a good pounding and add the sugar. Allow this to stand for 10 minutes so the sugar draws out some juice from the mint.

2 Give it another good pounding and stir in the red wine vinegar and oil.

3 Transfer to a small serving jug with a teaspoon to serve.

SWEET CHILLI SAUCE

Simple but effective. If you don't have a blender just chop everything finely and whisk together.

INGREDIENTS

MAKES A JAR FULL

A thumb-sized piece of ginger
1 jar of redcurrant jelly
1 whole red chilli
1 clove of garlic, peeled
1 tablespoon malt vinegar

METHOD

1 Peel the ginger and chop it roughly.

2 Put all ingredients into a blender and whiz up for 1 minute.

3 Wash out a suitable-sized jar and fill with boiling water to sterilise. When dried pour the sauce into the jar and refrigerate. It will keep for two weeks in the fridge.

MULLED WINE

There is nothing like the smell of mulled wine about the house to really get me into a Christmas mood. It just fills the house with every scent that sums up that time of year. When the weather outside is frightful, then a glass of this will warm the cockles of your heart. There is no point in boiling the life out of your wine and boiling off the alcohol, so that's why it is best to make a syrup at the start, then add the rest of the wine to it and just heat it up to drinking temperature.

INGREDIENTS

3–4 clementines
1 lemon
1 lime
275g caster sugar
2 bottles of good red wine
6 cloves
1 cinnamon stick
3 cardamom pods
3 bay leaves
2 star anise
1 teaspoon vanilla essence
1 nutmeg

MAKES 2 BOTTLES

METHOD

1 With a vegetable peeler, peel large sections off the skin of the clementines, lemon and lime. Put these in a large pot. Squeeze the juice of the clementines, lemon and lime into the pot. Add the sugar and a glass of the red wine and turn up the heat.

2 Add the cloves, cinnamon, cardamom pods, bay leaves, one of the star anise, the vanilla essence and grate in the nutmeg.

3 Stir well and bring to the boil, then boil rapidly for about 5 minutes, or until thickened. Turn the heat down to half and add in the rest of the wine along with the second star anise.

4 When heated fully, keep it warm and ladle out into glasses to serve. (If topping up with more wine, remember to add more sugar to taste.)

PASTA

Home-made pasta is simple when you get into the swing of it. A pasta roller machine won't set you back much at all and will make life so much easier. Yes it is much simpler to go and buy pasta in the shops, but this is fun to do! Plus it is a great workout for the forearms — Italian mama's would be proud!

INGREDIENTS

140g strong flour or pasta flour
1 large egg, plus 1 egg yolk

MAKES 3–4 PORTIONS FOR SPAGHETTI OR 1 LARGE LASAGNE

METHOD

1 Mix the ingredients together in a bowl or a food processor until it resembles fine breadcrumbs (it shouldn't look wet or too dusty, you can adjust this either way with the addition of a little water or a sprinkle of flour respectively).

2 Tip the mixture out onto a work surface and form it into a ball; stick with it, it will come together.

3 Knead the ball briskly for 1–2 minutes (it will be quite stiff) and wrap in cling film and place in the fridge for 1 hour.

4 After the hour, cut the dough in half and roll one half out to a 5mm/¼in thick square and put it through a pasta machine at the widest setting – setting number seven on mine. Fold it in half.

5 Put it through again at this setting, folding in half again, repeat this another five times at this setting.

6 Now you can start reducing the settings: however, this time don't fold it over and put it through each setting only once. Repeat the process until you have reached the thinnest setting. Repeat for the second half of the dough.

7 You can trim these sheets to suit the size of your lasagne dish; there also will be a cutter attachment on the machine for making spaghetti.

8 Cook your spaghetti in boiling water until al dente (usually 4–6 mins).

PESTO

There are certain things that can be bought pre-made for our convenience that taste wonderful. Then there are some things that, when home-made, would beat hands down anything that mass production could even dream of producing ... pesto is one of the latter. Some things are worth a little time and effort. This is a very basic and standard recipe, but once you make your own you will taste the difference. Pesto can be used in a host of recipe ideas, added into pasta dishes, spread on bruschetta, it is a beautiful accompaniment for grilled chicken or pork, toss your steamed vegetables in it ... the list really does go on and on.

INGREDIENTS

A small handful of pine nuts
¼ clove of garlic, peeled
Pinch of sea salt
An extra-large bunch of basil
A small handful of grated Parmesan cheese
Extra virgin olive oil
Black pepper to season

FEEDS 4

METHOD

1 Lightly toast the pine nuts on a small, dry frying pan over a medium/high heat. Shake them around and don't colour them too much.

2 Place the garlic, salt and picked leaves from the basil in a food processor.

3 Give it a good blitz until finely chopped. Add in the pine nuts and blitz again.

4 Scoop out the contents into a mixing bowl, add in three-quarters of the grated Parmesan cheese and stir it in while drizzling in the oil until you have an oozy mix.

5 Add a generous pinch of freshly crushed black pepper and taste. Adjust seasoning if need be.

6 Add in the rest of the Parmesan cheese and more oil until you have reached the consistency you desire. Continue to taste – this is your pesto, it should taste how you like it!

SIMPLE SHORTCRUST PASTRY

This pastry can be made by hand, but in a food processor it's made within a few minutes. In the kitchen we should always try and make life a little easier on ourselves!

MAKES 1 x 9in/23cm BASE

INGREDIENTS

125g plain flour
A pinch of salt
55g cubed butter
2–3 tablespoons cold water

METHOD

1 Place the flour, salt and butter into the food processor and pulse until the butter is fully mixed through and it looks like fine breadcrumbs. With the motor still running, pour the water in bit by bit until it just forms a dough.

2 Remove it from the mixer and wrap in cling film. Chill for at least 20 minutes before rolling out with a rolling pin.

3 For a sweet variation of this recipe, do not add the pinch of salt, instead, sift in 25g of icing sugar and add a further 20g of butter.

4 To pre-cook a pastry case it is 'blind baked'. Preheat the oven to 160°C. Roll out the dough larger than the diameter of your pre-greased tin. Carefully roll it back up onto the rolling pin and then roll it out over the top of the tin. Gently push it down so that it is in full contact with the whole tin – you can trim the excess overhang after it is baked. Then gently prick the pastry all over with a fork to help stop it rising. Cut a piece of parchment paper, again larger than the tin and lay this on top. Pour in ceramic baking beads to weigh the pastry down so it won't rise or swell. Bake for 25 mins in the oven, then carefully remove the beads and finish baking for a further 5 mins. Once out, and while still hot, trim off the excess overhang and allow the base to cool.

YOGURT

There is something great about making home-made yogurt. I don't make it as often as I'd like to, but when I do I just love it. It is thinner than shop-bought yogurt but is perfect for using in home-made smoothies or to pour over cereal or fresh fruit. You can thicken it up by adding dried skimmed milk powder to the milk, but I think that's unnecessary. When using live natural yogurt to start it off, make sure the container says 'Live' on it, so there is a live bacterium in it that turns the milk to yogurt.

INGREDIENTS   MAKES 500ml

500ml whole milk
2–3 tablespoons live natural yogurt

METHOD

1 Make sure everything you use to make yogurt is super clean so you don't grow the wrong kind of bacteria: place a whisk, saucepan, tablespoon, thermometer and mixing bowl in the sink. Boil a full kettle and pour it over everything in the sink to sterilise it. Turn on the cold tap and cool the items off and just shake dry.

2 Pour the milk into a saucepan and place on a medium heat. Place the thermometer into the saucepan and watch it like a hawk while stirring the milk gently. When the temperature reaches 46°C, take the saucepan off the heat and pour the milk into the mixing bowl.

3 Making sure the temperature hasn't gone above 46°C, whisk in the yogurt so that it blends with the milk.

4 Cover the bowl with cling film and wrap it in a clean towel. Place the wrapped bowl into a warm place, such as an airing cupboard. Check the yogurt after 6–8 hours or even overnight. If it still looks very runny leave it another few hours. If it has thickened, then place into the fridge and chill before use.

THANK YOU

I feel totally humbled by the fact that I am now writing my thank you page for my book. This whole project has been five years in the making. I had no idea where it would end up, but I did know I had a purpose, something big to strive towards. I had countless doors closed in my face and, with hindsight, for very good reason. Some of my ideas had been a little unorthodox to say the least. I wouldn't say that I never gave up, because I gave up on numerous occasions, but that didn't stop me from starting over again and, well, here I am.

Thank you mum: your support, advice and belief in me, even when I was scraping the floors for inspiration to make a life for myself, have been second to none. Being the youngest of nine I always say in jest that you kept going until you reached perfection, where in reality, the truth is, you had nine of us because your heart was big enough to love us all unconditionally. I love you.

My sisters Michele, Siobhan, Majella, Louise and Andrea, my brothers John, Anthony and Carl: you all have played a part in this, either directly or indirectly, but I have taken parts of all of you and used them in my life; you aren't all as useless as I make out! ☺

Thank you Ciara and the Behan's for all your support and love over the struggling years, I deeply appreciated it all.

A huge thank you to all the staff at Mercier Press, for believing I had something to offer and for going along with my visions … well some of them anyway. ☺

Amy, for everything — and I mean everything — I wouldn't even know where to start, amazing xx! And to Brendan for the patience and skill to have me looking half well for the cover shot, even though the stilts didn't get a look in …

To all my other friends, family, neighbours (a special mention to Mary, you listened to every idea; you have the patience of a saint girl).

And my greatest inspiration, a true gentleman, my dad — missed and loved always. I hope you can see this!

This is only the beginning!

INDEX OF RECIPES

H

HOME-MADE ALTERNATIVES

L

LUNCH

S

SIDES

SOUPS AND CHOWDERS

STARTERS